APPLETON-CENTURY PHILOSOPHY SOURCE-BOOKS
STERLING P. LAMPRECHT, *Editor*

D1155780

SELECTIONS FROM

BERGSON

SELECTIONS FROM
BERGSON

Edited with An Introduction by

HAROLD A. LARRABEE

Ichabod Spencer Professor of Philosophy
Union College

APPLETON-CENTURY-CROFTS, INC.

New York

PRINTED IN THE UNITED STATES OF AMERICA

E 08655

CONTENTS

* The two dates are those of the years of first publication in French and in English respectively.

INTRODUCTION

"There is a thinker whose name is today on everybody's lips, who is deemed by acknowledged philosophers worthy of comparison with the greatest, and who, with his pen as well as his brain, has overleapt all technical obstacles, and won himself a reading both outside and inside the schools. Beyond any doubt, and by common consent, Mr. Henri Bergson's work will appear to future eyes among the most characteristic, fertile, and glorious of our era. It marks a never-to-be-forgotten date in history; it opens up a phase of metaphysical thought; it lays down a principle of development the limits of which are indeterminable; and it is after cool consideration, with full consciousness of the exact value of words, that we are able to pronounce the revolution which it effects equal in importance to that effected by Kant, or even by Socrates." [1]

These glowing words from the pen of Bergson's colleague and compatriot Édouard Le Roy are cited not only to illustrate once more the fallibility of human prophecy, but also to convey a sense of the remoteness of the era of which he speaks. Two world wars have thrown an almost impenetrable smoke-screen between ourselves and those sun-lit days of the first thirteen years of the twentieth century, when Henri Bergson was at the summit of his popularity. For a few short years, from the publication of *Creative Evolution* in 1907 through

[1] Édouard Le Roy, *The New Philosophy of Henri Bergson* (New York, Henry Holt and Co., 1913), pp. 1-2.

his visit to America to lecture at Columbia University in 1912–13, he enjoyed a vogue surpassing that of any modern philosopher. So many Parisian ladies of fashion stormed his lecture-room at the Collège de France that several rows of seats had to be reserved in order to accomodate mere students. His works stirred William James to the point of ecstasy; and library tables and shelves were soon littered with commentaries pro and con, all the way from *Bergson for Beginners* to highly technical treatises. A new day in philosophy, and not in philosophy only, seemed to many to have dawned, with Bergson as its rising sun. The woods were full of Bergsonians: in literature, Bernard Shaw and Marcel Proust (who had been Bergson's best man at the latter's wedding); in politics, Georges Sorel; in religion, Jacques Maritain; in painting, Claude Monet; and in music, Claude Debussy. A philosopher who used the language of science like an inspired poet was just what the world had been waiting for, or so it seemed in 1907–13.

There are many reasons why it is difficult for us to recover the excitement, let alone the flaring enthusiasm, which Bergson aroused in that far-off and ignorantly happy time. To those who listened to his lectures and read his books, he appeared as a liberator sent to rescue mankind from the chains of scientific rationalism, a champion of creativity and freedom in a world which seemed threatened by the ogres of materialism and determinism. To all who believed themselves hemmed in by logic or formulas or the cake of custom, Bergson spoke in terms of fluidity and spontaneity and release. "Always follow your inspiration" was his welcome advice. Yet here was no wild romantic, but only too apparently a superbly gifted intellectual who harped incessantly upon the dangers of the intellect, and on the superior virtues of that *élan vital* of which intellect can be, at best, only the blundering instrument in its dealings with material things. Philosophers are still debating whether Bergson's philosophy as a whole deserves the epithets "irrational" or "anti-intellectual" which some have applied to it. But the mere suspicion that those tags are not wholly inappropriate is enough to put us on our guard.

For we, unlike Bergson's earlier readers, are survivors of the Axis onslaught of 1939–45. In 1907, the enemy appeared to be what William James called "the beast, Intellectualism," and as against it, and all manner of nineteenth-century scientific and social rigidities, vitality and animal vigor had much in their favor. When Bergson attacked all the dead hands which close in upon the living, he spoke for the romantic rebel in all of us. But far worse beasts than intellectualism, overflowing, too, with savage vitality, have since come forth; and praise of blind instinct at the apparent expense of intelligent discrimination has a hollow ring indeed to those who have witnessed the abominations committed by the fanatics who boasted that they "thought with their blood."

This is not to accuse Bergson of the slightest sympathy with the instinct-trusting madmen who embittered his own last years on earth. For he not only had the misfortune to outlive the period of his greatest influence, but to live on and on while his beloved France went down into the pit of an inconceivable defeat. Two acts of rare courage, in a life whose very living had become an act of courage, marked his final days: several weeks before his death at the age of eighty-one he rose from the sick-bed which had been his abode for years, and, in a bathrobe and on the arm of a servant, stood in a queue in order to register as a Jew. Before that, he had publicly refused exemption from the infamous laws of the Vichy government barring Jews from holding educational posts in France, as well as renouncing all the honors he had received whose retention might be construed as approval of the regime.

After Bergson's death, the claim was made by some of his more ardent Catholic friends that he had taken the final step from complete assimilation to conversion and baptism at a time and place unknown. The matter may, however, be considered to have been settled, once and for all, by the following letter from his widow to M. Emmanuel Mounier, published in the *Gazette de Lausanne* on September 9, 1941:

"My husband, who had given his attention for a long time to the problem of religion, especially after the publication of *Two Sources* in 1932, considered Catholicism with an increasing sympathy, but nevertheless did not wish to become a convert for several diverse reasons which some of his close friends, with whom he had discussed the matter in all frankness, understood and approved. He himself explained the matter with great clearness in a passage in his will, dated February 8, 1937, which I think I ought to communicate to you.

'My reflections have led me closer and closer to Catholicism, in which I see the complete fulfillment of Judaism. I would have become a convert, had I not foreseen for years a formidable wave of anti-Semitism about to break upon the world. I wanted to remain among those who tomorrow were to be persecuted. But I hope that a Catholic priest will consent, if the Cardinal Archbishop of Paris will authorize it, to come to say prayers at my funeral. In case that authorization is not granted, a rabbi should be invited to do so, without concealing from him or from anyone my moral adherence to Catholicism, or my preference for the prayers of a Catholic priest.'

"The intent of Henri Bergson, which was very clearly apparent, permits of no divergence of interpretation. At the same time that he declared his 'moral adherence' to Catholicism, my husband determined never to take the decisive step of baptism. It would be a poor way of paying tribute to his total loyalty to what he thought was the truth, to attribute to him acts which he never intended to commit while he was living, and to inflect his thought, now that he is no longer here to correct errors and to defend himself, in a sense which, whatever may be the motive, cannot help but singularly denature it."

But this was not all. His widow had the further misfortune, at the time of his death on January 4, 1941, to receive an official message of condolence from the then-Secretary of State for Education of the Pétain government, Professor Jacques Chevalier of the University of Grenoble, a brilliant Catholic disciple of Bergson's, condemned after the liberation to twenty years at hard labor and national unworthiness for life, extolling his former master as "a forerunner and an artisan of the French renaissance" (so-called) of 1940. To crown disgrace with undeserved disgrace, the French nation which Bergson had served with such faithfulness and distinction was represented at his funeral, attended only by some thirty persons, by Ambassador de Brinon! Paul Valéry, it should be added, made some amends for these disasters to Bergson's memory by his moving and defiant eulogy, ending with these words: "Most high, most pure, most superior figure of a thinking man, and perhaps one of the last men who has thought exclusively, profoundly, and exaltedly in an epoch when men think less and less, when civilization seems from day to day to be reducing itself to memories and vestiges of its multiform riches and its free and superabundant intellectual productivity, while misery, anguish, and

constraints of every variety depress and discourage enterprises of the mind, Bergson seems already to belong to an
age that is past, and his name seems to be the last great name
of the European intellect."

But the life which ended thus amid the darkness and confusion of the Third Republic's debacle had had its bright beginning when the Second Empire of Napoleon III was at
the height of its prosperity and power. Henri-Louis Bergson
was born at Paris on October 18, 1859. His father, Michael
Bergson (1818–98) was a talented and widely-traveled musi-
cian, an admirer of Chopin and himself a composer, who
headed the Geneva Conservatory for a time, and married
an English Jewess, Katherine Levinson. He was one of three
brothers, sons of Berek (whence the name Bergson, from
Berek-son), a wealthy and privileged trader noted for his
charities, whose father Samuel Zbitkower was "a rich War-
saw Jew, with typical beard and earlocks, and dressed in a
long silken cloak gathered in by a woven girdle." It was this
Samuel, Bergson's great-grandfather, who acquired such
wealth by trading and by shipping grain on rafts down the
Vistula to Danzig that he was given the official "privilege"
of dwelling in localities forbidden to other Jews.

With a cosmopolitan artist father, an English mother, and
French birth and schooling, Henri Bergson became so wholly
assimilated that he thought of himself simply as French.
When queried about Zionism by Herman Bernstein in 1912,
he replied: "To us French people this question seems paradoxical. We are so completely assimilated. If there were a
new Zion, I do not think many Jews would go there. . . ." A
few critics, some with less than friendly intent, have sought
to find traces of Jewish influence in his thought. To them he
stated wryly in 1910: "I should willingly admit my ideas to

be Jewish, but the misfortune is that I am not at all sure of it. Or rather, I am certain of profound obligation to only two or three philosophers, none of whom is Jewish: Plotinus, Maine de Biran, and somewhat to Ravaisson." [1]

In a letter to William James, Bergson summed up his *curriculum vitae* in just eight lines; and added: "Now as to events worthy of note, there have been none in the course of my career,—at least nothing *objectively* remarkable." Yet his record from the age of nine, when he entered the Lycée Condorcet, was an unbroken succession of academic triumphs and awards in a great variety of competitions. At nineteen he shocked his admiring teacher of mathematics Desboves by electing to compete for admission to the École Normale Supérieure in letters instead of science. He promptly distinguished himself as a Greek scholar; and in the final rankings of the *agrégation* he was second only to Jean Jaurès. Being qualified to teach, he began his career in 1881 as professor of philosophy at the lycée in Angers. After two years, he moved to a similar position at the Lycée Blaise Pascal in Clermont-Ferrand. It was there that an important *subjective* change took place. As he wrote to James: "I had remained up to that time wholly imbued with mechanistic theories, to which I had been led at an early date by the reading of Herbert Spencer. . . . It was the analysis of the notion of time, as that enters into mechanics and physics, which overturned all my ideas. I saw, to my great astonishment, that scientific time does not *endure* . . . that positive science consists essentially in the elimination of duration. This was the point of departure of a series of reflections which brought me, by

[1] Ben-Ami Scharfstein, *Roots of Bergson's Philosophy* (New York, Columbia University Press, 1943), p. 100. The details about Bergson's ancestry are from this source.

gradual steps, to reject almost all of what I had hitherto accepted and to change my point of view completely." [1]

From this key-idea, that the mathematical concept of time takes no account of real duration, the very stuff of our psychological existence, given to us immediately in consciousness, came one of the most famous of all doctoral theses, the *Essai sur les données immédiates de la conscience,* written at Clermont and published in 1889. A year earlier, Bergson had returned to his native Paris at the Collège Rollin, and then at the Lycée Henri IV, where he expanded his psychological researches (it took him five years merely to scrutinize the literature of aphasia) to the field of biology in his *Matière et mémoire,* which appeared in 1896 to the immediate applause of only a few savants. In 1898 he began to give lectures at the École Normale Supérieure; and from 1900 to 1914 he was a professor at the Collège de France, being relieved of his active duties by Édouard Le Roy in 1914, although he continued to hold the chair until 1921, when he became honorary professor. Bergson was elected to the French Academy in 1914, but could not be received until the end of the war in 1918. The last twenty years of his life were heavily burdened with severe headaches and insomnia, preventing his return to the classroom. Nevertheless he served as the first president of that embryo UNESCO of its day, the Commission for Intellectual Coöperation of the League of Nations, making one of his last public appearances to preside over one of its plenary sessions in Paris in 1924, shortly before his resignation in 1925. On that occasion, Bergson, as always, seemed to incarnate French lucidity, precision, limpidity of style, *clarté,* combined with an extraordinary benignity and asceticism. In 1928 the Nobel Prize for literature crowned a career as

[1] Ralph Barton Perry, *The Thought and Character of William James* (Boston, Little, Brown and Co., 1935), Vol. II, p. 623.

author which had been continued in the classic *L'Evolution créatrice* in 1907, *L'Energie spirituelle* in 1919, and *Durée et simultanéité, à propos de la théorie d'Einstein* in 1922. His long-awaited book on ethics and religion, *Les Deux Sources de la morale et de la religion* came out in 1932, and represented quite literally the victory of his mind and will over paralyzing bouts of pain.

Stated with the starkest brevity, the main theme of Bergson's thought centers around his initial "taking of psychological time (*durée*) seriously" (in the phrase of Samuel Alexander) by an intuition that is free of analysis and particularly of space-bound number or measurement. Bergson is the modern Heraclitus pondering Zeno's paradoxes of the flying arrow and Achilles and the tortoise. Like all common-sense observers, he sees the arrow reach the mark, and Achilles overtake the tortoise. If the geometrizing intellect of Zeno the Eleatic says "Impossible!" then, replies Bergson, so much the worse for intellect and the static "things in space" which it presents to us. Once having accepted the inwardly-apprehended flux (a kind of *"Je dure donc je suis"*) as the basis of his philosophical method, Bergson went on to apply it to physics, biology, psychology, aesthetics, ethics and religion. In each field of inquiry, as he repeatedly remarked, he endeavored to follow the contours and the sinuosities of the flowing, changing subject-matter which he encountered.

As a result, Bergson's works are, each of them, systematic; but his writings do not form a philosophical system in the ordinary sense of the term. They have often been compared to a grandiose musical composition, a kind of super-symphony, developed in many unpredictable directions from a few relatively simple themes. Anything like a completely sympathetic appreciation of the subtlety of Bergson's rhythmical elaboration of these themes requires a complete read-

ing of his entire output in chronological order, and prefer-
ably in French. For it is his central thesis that reality,
including, of course, his own philosophy, must be grasped
from within by an act of intuition, and not by the piecing
together of externally related bits. This makes the venture
of presenting selections from Bergson in English more than
usually perilous. It might even be pointed out that Bergson
himself has warned us against any such attempt in the opening pages of his *Introduction to Metaphysics,* where he voices
his doubts that "all the translations of a poem into all possible
languages" could ever achieve "success in rendering the inner
meaning of the original." Luckily he knew English well
enough to supervise the authorized translations of his works
which were made during his lifetime, so that they may be
considered, at the very least, not to have misrepresented his
thought.

At the same time the attentive reader will perceive that
there are textual inconsistencies and alterations in the use of
terms in the course of the various selections, not all of which
are to be debited to the difficulties of translation. For Bergson,
the apostle of novelty and growth, was not ashamed to display evidences of his own inner development as his thinking
progressed. In that respect, in any event, he was consistent;
although it has often been said that his entire philosophical
enterprise constitutes an inconsistency: the use of intellect to
discredit intellect,—the application of a highly abstract
method of reasoning to the criticism of highly abstract reasoning as applied to life. Bergson, according to such critics,
should have confined himself to an intuitive, and not an intellectual, attack upon intellect, and to an intuitive defense
of his own intuitive position by means of the method of
poetry. What Bergson does is to supplement his wealth of
intellectual arguments with a varied and seemingly inex-

haustible fund of metaphor, such as his famous characteriza-
tion of the intellect as "cinematographical" in the closing
chapter of *Creative Evolution*. This would indicate that, in
practice, intellect and intuition are inextricably bound together, in spite of Bergson's efforts to separate them.

In defense of the present undertaking, however, it may
be said that many of the most valuable of Bergson's contributions to modern thought may be understood in translation
by anyone who will take the trouble to read selected passages
in order from his principal works. What needs most of all
to be guarded against by the beginner is the deceptive lucidity
of his style, the virtuosity which enchants and seduces the
reader, making him believe that he has achieved a painless
understanding of the most abstruse issues. Bergson does not
crusade or urge the acceptance of formulas or raise his voice.
With unvarying finesse he delicately suggests what looks like
a simple, metaphorical solution. His strategy is like that
which he attributes to life: insinuating itself humbly into
its milieu. But, in the end, things are seldom as simple as
Bergson's flowing eloquence has made them seem to be.
Selections which interrupt his arguments have at least the
advantage of refuting one charge brought against him: that
he secures assent to his conclusions by a process of hypnotiz-
ing his readers.

It is still too early to attempt to strike more than a trial-
balance of credits and debits in Bergson's account; and that
is something which each reader will want to do for himself
in any case. He is plainly one of the pioneer figures of the
"revolt against reason" in the late nineteenth-century mechanistic sense of the term. It does not detract from his originality to point out that he is a descendant of Heraclitus and
Plotinus and (as Höffding pointed out) Kierkegaard and
many others, with a French training and preference for the

"scientific" along with the supple and the living in philosophical thought. As he modestly remarked: "I have only
got rid of a certain number of ready-made ideas; I deserve
no great credit for it. I have tried to develop the taste for
introspection. But I have no system." [1] Now it so happened
that the ready-made ideas which he sought to clear away
were, in most instances, just those which presented the most
formidable obstacles to the acceptance of traditional religious
and moral beliefs. Consequently Bergson was hailed by many
of the general public and especially by some religious and
political zealots as their partial ally in the struggle against
the positivistic enlighteners. Whether intentionally or not,
as André Cresson points out, Bergson was credited with
having helped to restore man to the pedestal from which he
had fallen. In his early works, Bergson seemed torn, like
almost all the men of his age, between his scientific convic-
tions and his spiritual aspirations, and to be struggling hard
to reconcile them. But in *Two Sources* he abandons his previous largely naturalistic presuppositions and goes over to
the side of the mystic as against the scientist, identifying
reason with closed institutions and static concepts. The result
of exalting this vague sort of "openness" is to leave humanity
with no defenses against illusion, and hence at the mercy of
the first prophet with an absolute but indistinct inner as-
surance, unchecked by those hard-won tests of sanity that
have enabled us little by little to winnow the reliable insights
from the unreliable. Bergson is right in repeatedly reminding
us that it is not enough to see only the outsides of things; but
neither is it enough for tolerable social living to see only (or
primarily) what each of us believes to be the insides of things.
The very fact that Bergson's philosophy has been utilized
for their own purposes by the advocates of so many conflict-

[1] *Mercure de France*, Vol. XCIII (1911), p. 413.

ing causes is an indication that "open-endedness" has its perils.

To Bergson's everlasting credit must go his early perception (from within?) of the pervasive significance of process, change, activity, and evolution in modern thought. He must also be given high rank among the pragmatists in the sense that he helped mightily to make plain, once and for all, that action in some measure governs knowledge, as well as the reverse. Like his kindred spirit William James, Bergson had a keen sense of the sheer Protean *copiousness* of reality, and, as Ralph Barton Perry adds, "of the pathetic thinness of the concepts with which the human mind endeavors to represent it." His philosophy was a powerful corrective of genuine abuses in its day, but it did not bring about anything like the philosophical revolution anticipated by Le Roy. Scientists have gone on working just about as before, a little more conscious perhaps, of some of their limitations, but hardly convinced that their methods are fundamentally unsuitable for dealing with the whole of the real. Philosophers have moved on to other problems, or to a consideration of the same problems in other guises, and the quarrels of the schools continue unabated. Yet what John Dewey said of Bergson in 1912 still holds: "No philosophic problem will ever exhibit just the same face and aspect that it presented before Professor Bergson invited us to look at it in its connections with duration as a real and fundamental fact." The philosopher of the flux has merged with the flux, but the latter is not quite the same as before. Perhaps Bergson could ask for no better monument than the tribute of Jeanne Hersch of Geneva in the memorial volume assembled by Albert Béguin and Pierre Thévenaz: "It is Bergson, in a large measure, who has made us what we are."

HAROLD A. LARRABEE

AN INTRODUCTION TO METAPHYSICS [1]

Authorized Translation by T. E. Hulme

A comparison of the definitions of metaphysics and the various conceptions of the absolute leads to the discovery that philosophers, in spite of their apparent divergencies, agree in distinguishing two profoundly different ways of knowing a thing. The first implies that we move round the object; the second that we enter into it. The first depends on the point of view at which we are placed and on the symbols by which we express ourselves. The second neither depends on a point of view nor relies on any symbol. The first kind of knowledge may be said to stop at the *relative;* the second, in those cases where it is possible, to attain the *absolute.*

Consider, for example, the movement of an object in space. My perception of the motion will vary with the point of view, moving or stationary, from which I observe it. My expression of it will vary with the systems of axes, or the points of reference, to which I relate it; that is, with the symbols by which I translate it. For this double reason I call such motion *relative:* in the one case, as in the other, I am placed outside the object itself. But when I speak of an *absolute* movement, I am

[1] Essay first published in the *Revue de Métaphysique et de Morale* for January, 1903, four years before the appearance of *Creative Evolution.* Of the 92 pages of the 1912 edition in English, pages 1–48, 64–80, and 86–92 are included here. Omissions are invariably indicated by a row of dots. From *An Introduction to Metaphysics,* by Henri Bergson, trans. by T. E. Hulme. Copyright, 1912, by G. P. Putnam's Sons. Courtesy of G. P. Putnam's Sons.

attributing to the moving object an interior and, so to speak, states of mind; I also imply that I am in sympathy with those states, and that I insert myself in them by an effort of imagination. Then, according as the object is moving or stationary, according as it adopts one movement or another, what I experience will vary. And what I experience will depend neither on the point of view I may take up in regard to the object, since I am inside the object itself, nor on the symbols by which I may translate the motion, since I have rejected all translations in order to possess the original. In short, I shall no longer grasp the movement from without, remaining where I am, but from where it is, from within, as it is in itself. I shall possess an absolute.

Consider, again, a character whose adventures are related to me in a novel. The author may multiply the traits of his hero's character, may make him speak and act as much as he pleases, but all this can never be equivalent to the simple and indivisible feeling which I should experience if I were able for an instant to identify myself with the person of the hero himself. Out of that indivisible feeling, as from a spring, all the words, gestures, and actions of the man would appear to me to flow naturally. They would no longer be accidents which, added to the idea I had already formed of the character, continually enriched that idea, without ever completing it. The character would be given to me all at once, in its entirety, and the thousand incidents which manifest it, instead of adding themselves to the idea and so enriching it, would seem to me, on the contrary, to detach themselves from it, without, however, exhausting it or impoverishing its essence. All the things I am told about the man provide me with so many points of view from which I can observe him. All the traits which describe him, and which can make him known to me only by so many comparisons with persons or things I know already, are signs by which he is expressed more or less symbolically. Symbols and points of view, therefore, place me outside him; they give me only what he has in common with others, and not what belongs to him and to him alone. But that which is properly himself, that which constitutes his essence, cannot be perceived from without, being internal by definition, nor be expressed by symbols, being incommensurable with everything else. Description, history, and analysis leave me here in the relative. Coincidence with the person himself would alone give me the absolute.

It is in this sense, and in this sense only, that *absolute* is synonymous with *perfection*. Were all the photographs of a town, taken from all possible points of view, to go on indefinitely completing one another, they would never be equivalent to the solid town in which we walk about. Were all the translations of a poem into all possible languages to add together their various shades of meaning and, correcting each other by a kind of mutual retouching, to give a more and more faithful image of the poem they translate, they would yet never succeed in rendering the inner meaning of the original. A representation taken from a certain point of view, a translation made with certain symbols, will always remain imperfect in comparison with the object of which a view has been taken, or which the symbols seek to express. But the absolute, which is the object and not its representation, the original and not its translation, is perfect, by being perfectly what it is.

It is doubtless for this reason that the *absolute* has often been identified with the *infinite*. Suppose that I wished to communicate to some one who did not know Greek the extraordinarily simple impression that a passage in Homer makes upon me; I should first give a translation of the lines,

I should then comment on my translation, and then develop the commentary; in this way, by piling up explanation on explanation, I might approach nearer and nearer to what I wanted to express; but I should never quite reach it. When you raise your arm, you accomplish a movement of which you have, from within, a simple perception; but for me, watching it from the outside, your arm passes through one point, then through another, and between these two there will be still other points; so that, if I began to count, the operation would go on forever. Viewed from the inside, then, an absolute is a simple thing; but looked at from the outside, that is to say, relatively to other things, it becomes, in relation to these signs which express it, the gold coin for which we never seem able to finish giving small change. Now, that which lends itself at the same time both to an indivisible apprehension and to an inexhaustible enumeration is, by the very definition of the word, an infinite.

It follows from this that an absolute could only be given in an *intuition,* whilst everything else falls within the province of *analysis.* By intuition is meant the kind of *intellectual sympathy* by which one places oneself within an object in order to coincide with what is unique in it and consequently inexpressible. Analysis, on the contrary, is the operation which reduces the object to elements already known, that is, to elements common both to it and other objects. To analyze, therefore, is to express a thing as a function of something other than itself. All analysis is thus a translation, a development into symbols, a representation taken from successive points of view from which we note as many resemblances as possible between the new object which we are studying and others which we believe we know already. In its eternally unsatisfied desire to embrace the object around which it is compelled to turn, analysis multiplies without end the number of its points of view in order to complete its always incomplete representation, and ceaselessly varies its symbols that it may perfect the always imperfect translation. It goes on, therefore, to infinity. But intuition, if intuition is possible, is a simple act.

Now it is easy to see that the ordinary function of positive science is analysis. Positive science works, then, above all, with symbols. Even the most concrete of the natural sciences, those concerned with life, confine themselves to the visible form of living beings, their organs and anatomical elements. They make comparisons between these forms, they reduce the more complex to the more simple; in short, they study the workings of life in what is, so to speak, only its visual symbol. If there exists any means of possessing a reality absolutely instead of knowing it relatively, of placing oneself within it instead of looking at it from outside points of view, of having the intuition instead of making the analysis: in short, of seizing it without any expression, translation, or symbolic representation—metaphysics is that means. *Metaphysics, then, is the science which claims to dispense with symbols.*

* *
*

There is one reality, at least, which we all seize from within, by intuition and not by simple analysis. It is our own personality in its flowing through time—our self which endures. We may sympathize intellectually with nothing else, but we certainly sympathize with our own selves.

When I direct my attention inward to contemplate my own self (supposed for the moment to be inactive), I perceive at first, as a crust solidified on the surface, all the perceptions which come to it from the material world. These perceptions are clear, distinct, juxtaposed or juxtaposable one with another; they tend to group themselves into objects. Next, I notice the memories which more or less adhere to these perceptions and which serve to interpret them. These memories have been detached, as it were, from the depth of my personality, drawn to the surface by the perceptions which resemble them; they rest on the surface of my mind without being absolutely myself. Lastly, I feel the stir of tendencies and motor habits—a crown of virtual actions, more or less firmly bound to these perceptions and memories. All these clearly defined elements appear more distinct from me, the more distinct they are from each other. Radiating, as they do, from within outwards, they form, collectively, the surface of a sphere which tends to grow larger and lose itself in the exterior world. But if I draw myself in from the periphery towards the centre, if I search in the depth of my being that which is most uniformly, most constantly, and most enduringly myself, I find an altogether different thing.

There is, beneath these sharply cut crystals and this frozen surface, a continuous flux which is not comparable to any flux I have ever seen. There is a succession of states, each of which announces that which follows and contains that which precedes it. They can, properly speaking, only be said to form multiple states when I have already passed them and turn back to observe their track. Whilst I was experiencing them they were so solidly organized, so profoundly animated with a common life, that I could not have said where any one of them finished or where another commenced. In reality no one of them begins or ends, but all extend into each other.

This inner life may be compared to the unrolling of a coil, for there is no living being who does not feel himself coming gradually to the end of his rôle; and to live is to grow old. But it may just as well be compared to a continual rolling up, like that of a thread on a ball, for our past follows us, it swells incessantly with the present that it picks up on its way; and consciousness means memory.

But actually it is neither an unrolling nor a rolling up, for these two similes evoke the idea of lines and surfaces whose parts are homogeneous and superposable on one another. Now, there are no two identical moments in the life of the same conscious being. Take the simplest sensation, suppose it constant, absorb in it the entire personality: the consciousness which will accompany this sensation cannot remain identical with itself for two consecutive moments, because the second moment always contains, over and above the first, the memory that the first has bequeathed to it. A consciousness which could experience two identical moments would be a consciousness without memory. It would die and be born again continually. In what other way could one represent unconsciousness?

It would be better, then, to use as a comparison the myriad-tinted spectrum, with its insensible gradations leading from one shade to another. A current of feeling which passed along the spectrum, assuming in turn the tint of each of its shades, would experience a series of gradual changes, each of which would announce the one to follow and would sum up those which preceded it. Yet even here the successive shades of the spectrum always remain external one to another. They are juxtaposed; they occupy space. But pure duration, on the contrary, excludes all idea of juxtaposition, reciprocal externality, and extension.

Let us, then, rather, imagine an infinitely small elastic body, contracted, if it were possible, to a mathematical point. Let this be drawn out gradually in such a manner that from the point comes a constantly lengthening line. Let us fix our attention not on the line as a line, but on the action by which it is traced. Let us bear in mind that this action, in spite of its duration, is indivisible if accomplished without stopping, that if a stopping-point is inserted, we have two actions instead of one, that each of these separate actions is then the indivisible operation of which we speak, and that it is not the moving action itself which is divisible, but, rather, the stationary line it leaves behind it as its track in space. Finally, let us free ourselves from the space which underlies the movement in order to consider only the movement itself, the act of tension or extension; in short, pure mobility. We shall have this time a more faithful image of the development of our self in duration.

However, even this image is incomplete, and, indeed, every comparison will be insufficient, because the unrolling of our duration resembles in some of its aspects the unity of an advancing movement and in others the multiplicity of expanding states; and, clearly, no metaphor can express one of these two aspects without sacrificing the other. If I use the comparison of the spectrum with its thousand shades, I have before me a thing already made, whilst duration is continually in the making. If I think of an elastic which is being stretched, or of a spring which is extended or relaxed, I forget the richness of color, characteristic of duration that is lived, to see only the simple movement by which consciousness passes from one shade to another. The inner life is all this at once: variety of qualities, continuity of progress, and unity of direction. It cannot be represented by images.

But it is even less possible to represent it by *concepts,* that is by abstract, general, or simple ideas. It is true that no image can reproduce exactly the original feeling I have of the flow of my own conscious life. But it is not even necessary that I should attempt to render it. If a man is incapable of getting for himself the intuition of the constitutive duration of his own being, nothing will ever give it to him, concepts no more than images. Here the single aim of the philosopher should be to promote a certain effort, which in most men is usually fettered by habits of mind more useful to life. Now the image has at least this advantage, that it keeps us in the concrete. No image can replace the intuition of duration, but many diverse images, borrowed from very different orders of things, may, by the convergence of their action, direct consciousness to the precise point where there is a certain intuition to be seized. By choosing images as dissimilar as possible, we shall prevent any one of them from usurping the place of the intuition it is intended to call up, since it would then be driven away at once by its rivals. By providing that, in spite of their differences of aspect, they all require from the mind the same kind of attention, and in some sort the same degree of tension, we shall gradually accustom consciousness to a particular and clearly-defined disposition—that precisely which it must adopt in order to appear to itself as it really is, without any veil. But, then, consciousness must at least consent to make the effort. For it will have been shown nothing: it will simply have been placed in the attitude it must take up in order to make the desired effort, and so come by itself to the intuition. Concepts on the contrary—especially if they are simple—have the disadvantage of being in reality symbols substituted for the object they symbolize, and demand no effort on our part. Examined closely, each of them, it would be seen, retains only that part of the object which is common to it and to others, and expresses, still more than the image does, a *comparison* between the object and others which resemble it. But as the comparison has made manifest a resemblance, as the resemblance is a property of the object, and as a property has every appearance of being a *part* of the object which possesses it, we easily persuade ourselves that by setting concept beside concept we are reconstructing the whole of the object with its parts, thus obtaining, so to speak, its intellectual equivalent. In this way we believe that we can form a faithful representation of duration by setting in line the concepts of unity, multiplicity, continuity, finite or infinite divisibility, and so on. There precisely is the illusion. There also is the danger. Just in so far as abstract ideas can render service to analysis, that is, to the scientific study of the object in its relations to other objects, so far are they incapable of replacing intuition, that is, the metaphysical investigation of what is essential and unique in the object. For on the one hand these concepts, laid side by side, never actually give us more than an artificial reconstruction of the object, of which they can only symbolize certain general, and, in a way, impersonal aspects; it is therefore useless to believe that with them we can seize a reality of which they present to us the shadow alone. And, on the other hand, besides the illusion there is also a very serious danger. For the concept generalizes at the same time as it abstracts. The concept can only symbolize a particular property by making it common to an infinity of things. It therefore always more or less deforms the property by the extension it gives to it. Replaced in the metaphysical object to which it belongs, a property coincides with the object, or at least moulds itself on it, and adopts the same outline. Extracted from the metaphysical object, and presented in a concept, it grows indefinitely larger, and goes beyond the object itself, since henceforth it has to contain it, along with a number of other objects. Thus the different concepts that we form of the properties of a thing inscribe round it so many circles, each much too large and none of them fitting it exactly. And yet, in the thing itself the properties coincided with the thing, and coincided consequently with one another. So that if we are bent on reconstructing the object with concepts, some artifice must be sought whereby this coincidence of the object and its properties can be brought about. For example, we may choose one of the concepts and try, starting from it, to get round to the others. But we shall then soon discover that according as we start from one concept or another, the meeting and combination of the concepts will take place in an altogether different way. According as we start, for example, from unity or from multiplicity, we shall have to conceive differently the multiple unity of duration. Everything will depend on the weight we attribute to this or that concept, and this weight will always be arbitrary, since the concept extracted from the object has no weight, being only the shadow of a body. In this way, as many different *systems* will spring up as there are external points of view from which the reality can be examined, or larger circles in which it can be enclosed. Simple concepts have, then, not only the inconvenience of dividing the concrete unity of the object into so many symbolical expressions; they also divide philosophy into distinct schools, each of which takes its seat, chooses its counters, and carries on with the others a game that will never end. Either metaphysics is only this play of ideas, or else, if it is a serious occupation of the mind, if it is a science and not simply an exercise, it must transcend concepts in order to reach intuition. Certainly, concepts are necessary to it, for all the other sciences work as a rule with concepts, and metaphysics cannot dispense with the other sciences. But it is only truly itself when it goes beyond the concept, or at least when it frees itself from rigid and ready-made concepts in order to create a kind very different from those which we habitually use; I mean supple, mobile, and almost fluid representations, always ready to mould themselves on the fleeting forms of intuition. We shall return later to this important point. Let it suffice us for the moment to have shown that our duration can be presented to us directly in an intuition, that it can be suggested to us indirectly by images, but that it can never—if we confine the word concept to its proper meaning—be enclosed in a conceptual representation.

Let us try for an instant to consider our duration as a multiplicity. It will then be necessary to add that the terms of this multiplicity, instead of being distinct, as they are in any other multiplicity, encroach on one another; and that while we can no doubt, by an effort of imagination, solidify duration once it has elapsed, divide it into juxtaposed portions and count all these portions, yet this operation is accomplished on the frozen memory of the duration, on the stationary trace which the mobility of duration leaves behind it, and not on the duration itself. We must admit, therefore, that if there is a multiplicity here, it bears no resemblance to any other multiplicity we know. Shall we say, then, that duration has unity? Doubtless, a continuity of elements which prolong themselves into one another participates in unity as much as in multiplicity; but this moving, changing, colored, living unity has hardly anything in common with the abstract, motionless, and empty unity which the concept of pure unity circumscribes. Shall we conclude from this that duration must be defined as unity and multiplicity at the same time? But singularly enough, however much I manipulate the two concepts, portion them out, combine them differently, practice on them the most subtle operations of mental chemistry, I never obtain anything which resembles the simple intuition that I have of duration; while, on the contrary, when I replace myself in duration by an effort of intuition, I immediately perceive how it is unity, multiplicity, and many other things besides. These different concepts, then, were only so many standpoints from which we could consider duration. Neither separated nor reunited have they made us penetrate into it.

We do penetrate into it, however, and that can only be by an effort of intuition. In this sense, an inner, absolute knowledge of the duration of the self by the self is possible. But if metaphysics here demands and can obtain an intuition, science has none the less need of an analysis. Now it is a confusion between the function of analysis and that of intuition which gives birth to the discussions between the schools and the conflicts between systems.

Psychology, in fact, proceeds like all other sciences by analysis. It resolves the self, which has been given to it at first in a simple intuition, into sensations, feelings, ideas, and so on, which it studies separately. It substitutes, then, for the self a series of elements which form the facts of psychology. But are these *elements* really *parts?* That is the whole question, and it is because it has been evaded that the problem of human personality has so often been stated in insoluble terms.

It is incontestable that every psychical state, simply because it belongs to a person, reflects the whole of a personality. Every feeling, however simple it may be, contains virtually within it the whole past and present of the being experiencing it, and, consequently, can only be separated and constituted into a "state" by an effort of abstraction or of analysis. But it is no less incontestable that without this effort of abstraction or analysis there would be no possible development of the science of psychology. What, then, exactly, is the operation by which a psychologist detaches a mental state in order to erect it into a more or less independent entity? He begins by neglecting that special coloring of the personality which cannot be expressed in known and common terms. Then he endeavors to isolate, in the person already thus simplified, some aspect which lends itself to an interesting inquiry. If he is considering inclination, for example, he will neglect the inexpressible shade which colors it, and which makes the inclination mine and not yours; he will fix his attention on the movement by which our personality *leans towards* a certain object: he will isolate this attitude, and it is this special aspect of the personality, this snapshot of the mobility of the inner life, this "diagram" of concrete inclination, that he will erect into an independent fact. There is in this something very like what an artist passing through Paris does when he makes, for example, a sketch of a tower of Notre Dame. The tower is inseparably united to the building, which is itself no less inseparably united to the ground, to its surroundings, to the whole of Paris, and so on. It is first necessary to detach it from all these; only one aspect of the whole is noted, that formed by the tower of Notre Dame. Moreover, the special form of this tower is due to the grouping of the stones of which it is composed; but the artist does not concern himself with these stones, he notes only the silhouette of the tower. For the real and internal organization of the thing he substitutes, then, an external and schematic representation. So that, on the whole, his sketch corresponds to an observation of the object from a certain point of view and to the choice of a certain means of representation. But exactly the same thing holds true of the operation by which the psychologist extracts a single mental state from the whole personality. This isolated psychical state is hardly anything but a sketch, the commencement of an artificial reconstruction; it is the whole considered under a certain elementary aspect in which we are specially interested and which we have carefully noted. It is not a part, but an element. It has not been obtained by a natural dismemberment, but by analysis.

Now beneath all the sketches he has made at Paris the visitor will probably, by way of memento, write the word "Paris." And as he has really seen Paris, he will be able, with the help of the original intuition he had of the whole, to place his sketches therein, and so join them up together. But there is no way of performing the inverse operation; it is impossible, even with an infinite number of accurate sketches, and even with the word "Paris" which indicates that they must be combined together, to get back to an intuition that one has never had, and to give oneself an impression of what Paris is like if one has never seen it. This is because we are not dealing here with real *parts,* but with mere *notes* of the total impression. To take a still more striking example, where the notation is more completely symbolic, suppose that I am shown, mixed together at random, the letters which make up a poem I am ignorant of. If the letters were *parts* of the poem, I could attempt to reconstitute the poem with them by trying the different possible arrangements, as a child does with the pieces of a Chinese puzzle. But I should never for a moment think of attempting such a thing in this case, because the letters are not *component parts,* but only *partial expressions,* which is quite a different thing. That is why, if I know the poem, I at once put each of the letters in its proper place and join them up without difficulty by a continuous connection, whilst the inverse operation is impossible. Even when I believe I am actually attempting this inverse operation, even when I put the letters end to end, I begin by thinking of some plausible meaning. I thereby give myself an intuition, and from this intuition I attempt to redescend to the elementary symbols which would reconstitute its expression. The very idea of reconstituting a thing by operations practiced on symbolic elements alone implies such an absurdity that it would never occur to any one if they recollected that they were not dealing with fragments of the thing, but only, as it were, with fragments of its symbol.

Such is, however, the undertaking of the philosophers who try to reconstruct personality with psychical states, whether they confine themselves to those states alone, or whether they add a kind of thread for the purpose of joining the states together. Both empiricists and rationalists are victims of the same fallacy. Both of them mistake *partial notations* for *real parts,* thus confusing the point of view of analysis and of intuition, of science and of metaphysics.

The empiricists say quite rightly that psychological analysis discovers nothing more in personality than psychical states. Such is, in fact, the function, and the very definition of analysis. The psychologist has nothing else to do but analyze personality, that is, to note certain states; at the most he may put the label "ego" on these states in saying they are "states of the ego," just as the artist writes the word "Paris" on each of his sketches. On the level at which the psychologist places himself, and on which he must place himself, the "ego" is only a sign by which the primitive, and moreover very confused, intuition which has furnished the psychologist with his subject-matter is recalled; it is only a word, and the great error here lies in believing that while remaining on the same level we can find behind the word a thing. Such has been the error of those philosophers who have not been able to resign themselves to being only psychologists in psychology, Taine and Stuart Mill, for example. Psychologists in the method they apply, they have remained metaphysicians in the object they set before themselves. They desire an intuition, and by a strange inconsistency they seek this intuition in analysis, which is the very negation of it. They look for the ego, and they claim to find it in psychical states, though this diversity of states has itself only been obtained, and could only be obtained, by transporting oneself outside the ego altogether, so as to make a series of sketches, notes, and more or less symbolic and schematic diagrams. Thus, however much they place the states side by side, multiplying points of contact and exploring the intervals, the ego always escapes them, so that they finish by seeing in it nothing but a vain phantom. We might as well deny that the *Iliad* had a meaning, on the ground that we had looked in vain for that meaning in the intervals between the letters of which it is composed.

Philosophical empiricism is born here, then, of a confusion between the point of view of intuition and that of analysis. Seeking for the original in the translation, where naturally it cannot be, it denies the existence of the original on the ground that it is not found in the translation. It leads of necessity to negations; but on examining the matter closely, we perceive that these negations simply mean that analysis is not intuition, which is self-evident. From the original, and, one must add, very indistinct intuition which gives positive science its material, science passes immediately to analysis, which multiplies to infinity its observations of this material from outside points of view. It soon comes to believe that by putting together all these diagrams it can reconstitute the object itself. No wonder, then, that it sees this object fly before it, like a child that would like to make a solid plaything out of the shadows outlined along the wall!

But rationalism is the dupe of the same illusions. It starts out from the same confusion as empiricism, and remains equally powerless to reach the inner self. Like empiricism, it considers psychical states as so many fragments detached from an ego that binds them together. Like empiricism, it tries to join these fragments together in order to re-create the unity of the self. Like empiricism, finally, it sees this unity of the self, in the continually renewed effort it makes to clasp it, steal away indefinitely like a phantom. But whilst empiricism, weary of the struggle, ends by declaring that there is nothing else but the multiplicity of psychical states, rationalism persists in affirming the unity of the person. It is true that, seeking this unity on the level of the psychical states themselves, and obliged, besides, to put down to the account of these states all the qualities and determinations that it finds by analysis (since analysis by its very definition leads always to *states*), nothing is left to it, for the unity of personality, but something purely negative, the absence of all determination. The psychical states having necessarily in this analysis taken and kept for themselves everything that can serve as matter, the "unity of the ego" can never be more than a form without content. It will be absolutely indeterminate and absolutely void. To these detached psychical states, to these shadows of the ego, the sum of which was for the empiricists the equivalent of the self, rationalism, in order to reconstitute personality, adds something still more unreal, the void in which these shadows move—a place for shadows, one might say. How could this "form," which is in truth formless, serve to characterize a living, active, concrete personality, or to distinguish Peter from Paul? Is it astonishing that the philosophers who have isolated this "form" of personality should, then, find it insufficient to characterize a definite person, and that they should be gradually led to make their empty ego a kind of bottomless receptacle, which belongs no more to Peter than to Paul, and in which there is room, according to our preference, for entire humanity, for God, or for existence in general? I see in this matter only one difference between empiricism and rationalism. The former, seeking the unity of the ego in the gaps, as it were, between the psychical states, is led to fill the gaps with other states, and so on indefinitely, so that the ego, compressed in a constantly narrowing interval, tends towards zero, as analysis is pushed farther and farther; whilst rationalism, making the ego the place where mental states are lodged, is confronted with an empty space which we have no reason to limit here rather than there, which goes beyond each of the successive boundaries that we try to assign to it, which constantly grows larger, and which tends to lose itself no longer in zero, but in the infinite.

The distance, then, between a so-called "empiricism" like that of Taine and the most transcendental speculations of certain German pantheists is very much less than is generally supposed. The method is analogous in both cases; it consists in reasoning about the *elements* of a translation as if they were *parts* of the original. But a true empiricism is that which proposes to get as near to the original itself as possible, to search deeply into its life, and so, by a kind of *intellectual auscultation,* to feel the throbbings of its soul; and this true empiricism is the true metaphysics. It is true that the task is an extremely difficult one, for none of the ready-made conceptions which thought employs in its daily operations can be of any use. Nothing is more easy than to say that the ego is multiplicity, or that it is unity, or that it is the synthesis of both. Unity and multiplicity are here representations that we have no need to cut out on the model of the object; they are found ready-made, and have only to be chosen from a heap. They are stock-size clothes which do just as well for Peter as for Paul, for they set off the form of neither. But an empiricism worthy of the name, an empiricism which works only to measure, is obliged for each new object that it studies to make an absolutely fresh effort. It cuts out for the object a concept which is appropriate to that object alone, a concept which can as yet hardly be called a concept, since it applies to this one thing. It does not proceed by combining current ideas like unity and multiplicity; but it leads us, on the contrary, to a simple, unique representation, which, however once formed, enables us to understand easily how it is that we can place it in the frames unity, multiplicity, and so on, all much larger than itself. In short, philosophy thus defined does not consist in the choice of certain concepts, and in taking sides with a school, but in the search for a unique intuition from which we can descend with equal ease to different concepts, because we are placed above the divisions of the schools.

That personality has unity cannot be denied; but such an affirmation teaches one nothing about the extraordinary nature of the particular unity presented by personality. That our self is multiple I also agree, but then it must be understood that it is a multiplicity which has nothing in common with any other multiplicity. What is really important for philosophy is to know exactly what unity, what multiplicity, and what reality superior both to abstract unity and multiplicity the multiple unity of the self actually is. Now philosophy will know this only when it recovers possession of the simple intuition of the self by the self. Then, according to the direction it chooses for its descent from this summit, it will arrive at unity or multiplicity, or at any one of the concepts by which we try to define the moving life of the self. But no mingling of these concepts would give anything which at all resembles the self that endures.

If we are shown a solid cone, we see without any difficulty how it narrows towards the summit and tends to be lost in a mathematical point, and also how it enlarges in the direction of the base into an indefinitely increasing circle. But neither the point nor the circle, nor the juxtaposition of the two on a plane, would give us the least idea of a cone. The same thing holds true of the unity and multiplicity of mental life, and of the zero and the infinite towards which empiricism and rationalism conduct personality.

Concepts, as we shall show elsewhere, generally go together in couples and represent two contraries. There is hardly any concrete reality which cannot be observed from two opposing standpoints, which cannot consequently be subsumed under two antagonistic concepts. Hence a thesis and an antithesis which we endeavor in vain to reconcile logically, for the very simple reason that it is impossible, with concepts and observations taken from outside points of view, to make a thing. But from the object, seized by intuition, we pass easily in many cases to the two contrary concepts; and as in that way thesis and antithesis can be seen to spring from reality, we grasp at the same time how it is that the two are opposed and how they are reconciled.

It is true that to accomplish this, it is necessary to proceed by a reversal of the usual work of the intellect. *Thinking* usually consists in passing from concepts to things, and not from things to concepts. To know a reality, in the usual sense of the word "know," is to take ready-made concepts, to portion them out and to mix them together until a practical equivalent of the reality is obtained. But it must be remembered that the normal work of the intellect is far from being disinterested. We do not aim generally at knowledge for the sake of knowledge, but in order to take sides, to draw profit—in short, to satisfy an interest. We inquire up to what point the object we seek to know is *this* or *that,* to what known class it belongs, and what kind of action, bearing, or attitude it should suggest to us. These different possible actions and attitudes are so many *conceptual directions* of our thought, determined once for all; it remains only to follow them: in that precisely consists the application of concepts to things. To try to fit a concept on an object is simply to ask what we can do with the object, and what it can do for us. To label an object with a certain concept is to mark in precise terms the kind of action or attitude the object should suggest to us. All knowledge, properly so called, is then oriented in a certain direction, or taken from a certain point of view. It is true that our interest is often complex. This is why it happens that our knowledge of the same object may face several successive directions and may be taken from various points of view. It is this which constitutes, in the usual meaning of the terms, a "broad" and "comprehensive" knowledge of the object; the object is then brought not under one single concept, but under several in which it is supposed to "participate." How does it participate in all these concepts at the same time? This is a question which does not concern our practical action and about which we need not trouble. It is, therefore, natural and legitimate in daily life to proceed by the juxtaposition and portioning out of concepts; no philosophical difficulty will arise from this procedure, since by a tacit agreement we shall abstain from philosophizing. But to carry this *modus operandi* into philosophy, to pass here also from concepts to the thing, to use in order to obtain a disinterested knowledge of an object (that this time we desire to grasp as it is in itself) a manner of knowing inspired by a determinate interest, consisting by definition in an externally-taken view of the object, is to go against the end that we have chosen, to condemn philosophy to an eternal skirmishing between the schools and to install contradiction in the very heart of the object and of the method. Either there is no philosophy possible, and all knowledge of things is a practical knowledge aimed at the profit to be drawn from them, or else philosophy consists in placing oneself within the object itself by an effort of intuition.

But in order to understand the nature of this intuition, in

order to fix with precision where intuition ends and where analysis begins, it is necessary to return to what was said earlier about the flux of duration.

It will be noticed that an essential characteristic of the concepts and diagrams to which analysis leads is that, while being considered, they remain stationary. I isolate from the totality of interior life that psychical entity which I call a simple sensation. So long as I study it, I suppose that it remains constant. If I noticed any change in it, I should say that it was not a single sensation but several successive sensations, and I should then transfer to each of these successive sensations the immutability that I first attributed to the total sensation. In any case I can, by pushing the analysis far enough, always manage to arrive at elements which I agree to consider immutable. There, and there only, shall I find the solid basis of operations which science needs for its own proper development.

But, then, I cannot escape the objection that there is no state of mind, however simple, which does not change every moment, since there is no consciousness without memory, and no continuation of a state without the addition, to the present feeling, of the memory of past moments. It is this which constitutes duration. Inner duration is the continuous life of a memory which prolongs the past into the present, the present either containing within it in a distinct form the ceaselessly growing image of the past, or, more probably, showing by its continual change of quality the heavier and still heavier load we drag behind us as we grow older. Without this survival of the past into the present there would be no duration, but only instantaneity.

Probably if I am thus accused of taking the mental state out of duration by the mere fact that I analyze it, I shall reply, "Is not each of these elementary psychical states, to which my analysis leads, itself a state which occupies time? My analysis," I shall say, "does indeed resolve the inner life into states, each of which is homogeneous with itself; only, since the homogeneity extends over a definite number of minutes or of seconds, the elementry psychical state does not cease to endure, although it does not change."

But, in saying that, I fail to see that the definite number of minutes and of seconds, which I am attributing here to the elementary psychical state, has simply the value of a sign intended to remind me that the psychical state, supposed homogeneous, is in reality a state which changes and endures. The state, taken in itself, is a perpetual becoming. I have extracted from this becoming a certain average of quality, which I have supposed invariable; I have in this way constituted a stable and consequently schematic state. I have, on the other hand, extracted from it Becoming in general, *i.e.,* a becoming which is not the becoming of any particular thing, and this is what I have called the *time* the state occupies. Were I to look at it closely, I should see that this abstract time is as immobile for me as the state which I localize in it, that it could flow only by a continual change of quality, and that if it is without quality, merely the theatre of the change, it thus becomes an immobile medium. I should see that the construction of this homogeneous time is simply designed to facilitate the comparison between the different concrete durations, to permit us to count simultaneities, and to measure one flux of duration in relation to another. And lastly I should understand that, in attaching the sign of a definite number of minutes and of seconds to the representation of an elementary psychical state, I am merely reminding myself and others that the state has been detached from an ego which endures, and merely marking out the place where it must again be set in movement in order to bring it back from the abstract schematic thing it has become to the concrete state it was at first. But I ignore all that, because it has nothing to do with analysis.

This means that analysis operates always on the immobile, whilst intuition places itself in mobility, or, what comes to the same thing, in duration. There lies the very distinct line of demarcation between intuition and analysis. The real, the experienced, and the concrete are recognized by the fact that they are variability itself, the element by the fact that it is invariable. And the element is invariable by definition, being a diagram, a simplified reconstruction, often a mere symbol, in any case a motionless view of the moving reality.

But the error consists in believing that we can reconstruct the real with these diagrams. As we have already said and may as well repeat here—from intuition one can pass to analysis, but not from analysis to intuition.

Out of variability we can make as many variations, qualities and modifications as we please, since these are so many static views, taken by analysis, of the mobility given to intuition. But these modifications, put end to end, will produce nothing which resembles variability, since they are not parts of it, but elements, which is quite a different thing.

. . . having presented a general view of the method and made a first application of it, it may not be amiss to formulate, as precisely as we can, the principles on which it rests. Most of the following propositions have already received in this essay some degree of proof. We hope to demonstrate them more completely when we come to deal with other problems.

I. *There is a reality that is external and yet given immediately to the mind*. Common-sense is right on this point, as against the idealism and realism of the philosophers.

II. This reality is mobility. Not *things* made, but things in the making, not self-maintaining *states,* but only changing states, exist. Rest is never more than apparent, or, rather, relative. The consciousness we have of our own self in its continual flux introduces us to the interior of a reality, on the model of which we must represent other realities. *All reality, therefore, is tendency, if we agree to mean by tendency an incipient change of direction.*

III. Our mind, which seeks for solid points of support, has for its main function in the ordinary course of life that of representing *states* and *things.* It takes, at long intervals, almost instantaneous views of the undivided mobility of the real. It thus obtains *sensations* and *ideas.* In this way it substitutes for the continuous the discontinuous, for motion stability, for tendency in process of change, fixed points marking a direction of change and tendency. This substitution is necessary to common-sense, to language, to practical life, and even, in a certain degree, which we shall endeavor to determine, to positive science. *Our intellect, when it follows its natural bent, proceeds on the one hand by solid perceptions, and on the other by stable conceptions.* It starts from the immobile, and only conceives and expresses movement as a function of immobility. It takes up its position in ready-made concepts, and endeavors to catch in them, as in a net, something of the reality which passes. This is certainly not done in order to obtain an internal and metaphysical knowledge of the real, but simply in order to utilize the real, each concept (as also each sensation) being a *practical question* which our activity puts to reality and to which reality replies, as must be done in business, by a Yes or a No. But, in doing that, it lets that which is its very essence escape from the real.

IV. The inherent difficulties of metaphysic, the antinomies which it gives rise to, and the contradictions into which it falls, the division into antagonistic schools, and the irreducible opposition between systems are largely the result of our applying, to the disinterested knowledge of the real, processes which we generally employ for practical ends. They arise from the fact that we place ourselves in the immobile in order to lie in wait for the moving thing as it passes, instead of replacing ourselves in the moving thing itself, in order to traverse with it the immobile positions. They arise from our professing to reconstruct reality—which is tendency and consequently mobility—with percepts and concepts whose function it is to make it stationary. With stoppages, however numerous they may be, we shall never make mobility; whereas, if mobility is given, we can, by means of diminution, obtain from it by thought as many stoppages as we desire. In other words, *it is clear that fixed concepts may be extracted by our thought from mobile reality; but there are no means of reconstructing the mobility of the real with fixed concepts.* Dogmatism, however, in so far as it has been a builder of systems, has always attempted this reconstruction.

V. In this it was bound to fail. It is on this impotence and on this impotence only that the sceptical, idealist, critical doctrines really dwell: in fact, all doctrines that deny to our intelligence the power of attaining the absolute. But because we fail to reconstruct the living reality with stiff and ready-made concepts, it does not follow that we cannot grasp it in some other way. *The demonstrations which have been given of the relativity of our knowledge are therefore tainted with an original vice; they imply, like the dogmatism they attack, that all knowledge must necessarily start from concepts with fixed outlines, in order to clasp with them the reality which flows.*

VI. But the truth is that our intelligence can follow the opposite method. It can place itself within the mobile reality, and adopt its ceaselessly changing direction; in short, can grasp it by means of that *intellectual sympathy* which we can intuition. This is extremely difficult. The mind has to do violence to itself, has to reverse the direction of the operation by which it habitually thinks, has perpetually to revise, or rather to recast, all its categories. But in this way it will attain to fluid concepts, capable of following reality in all its sinuosities and of adopting the very movement of the inward life of things. Only thus will a progressive philosophy be built up, freed from the disputes which arise between the various schools, and able to solve its problems naturally, because it will be released from the artificial expression in terms of which such problems are posited. *To philosophize, therefore, is to invert the habitual direction of the work of thought.*

VII. This inversion has never been practiced in a methodical manner; but a profoundly considered history of human thought would show that we owe to it all that is greatest in the sciences, as well as all that is permanent in metaphysics. The most powerful of the methods of investigation at the disposal of the human mind, the infinitesimal calculus, originated from this very inversion. Modern mathematics is precisely an effort to substitute the *being made* for the *ready made,* to follow the generation of magnitudes, to grasp motion no longer from without and in its displayed result, but from within and in its tendency to change; in short, to adopt the mobile continuity of the outlines of things. It is true that it is confined to the outline, being only the science of magnitudes. It is true also that it has only been able to achieve its marvelous applications by the invention of certain symbols, and that if the intuition of which we have just spoken lies at the origin of invention, it is the symbol alone which is concerned in the application. But metaphysics, which aims at no application, can and usually must abstain from converting intuition into symbols. Liberated from the obligation of working for practically useful results, it will indefinitely enlarge the domain of its investigations. What it may lose in comparison with science in utility and exactitude, it will regain in range and extension. Though mathematics is only the science of magnitudes, though mathematical processes are applicable only to quantities, it must not be forgotten that quantity is always quality in a nascent state; it is, we might say, the limiting case of quality. It is natural, then, that metaphysics should adopt the generative idea of our mathematics in order to extend it to all qualities; that is, to reality in general. It will not, by doing this, in any way be moving towards universal mathematics, that chimera of modern philosophy. On the contrary, the farther its goes, the more untranslatable into symbols will be the objects it encounters. But it will at least have begun by getting into contact with the continuity and mobility of the real, just where this contact can be most marvelously utilized. It will have contemplated itself in a mirror which reflects an image of itself, much shrunken, no doubt, but for that reason very luminous. It will have seen with greater clearness what the mathematical processes borrow from concrete reality, and it will continue in the direction of concrete reality, and not in that of mathematical processes. Having then discounted beforehand what is too modest, and at the same time too ambitious, in the following formula, we may say that *the object of metaphysics is to perform* qualitative *differentiations and integrations.*

VIII. The reason why this object has been lost sight of, and why science itself has been mistaken in the origin of the processes it employs, is that intuition, once attained, must find a mode of expression and of application which conforms to the habits of our thought, and one which furnishes us, in the shape of well-defined concepts, with the solid points of support which we so greatly need. In that lies the condition of what we call exactitude and precision, and also the condition of the unlimited extension of a general method to particular cases. Now this extension and this work of logical improvement can be continued for centuries, whilst the act which creates the method lasts but for a moment. That is why we so often take the logical equipment of science for science itself,[1] forgetting the metaphysical intuition from which all the rest has sprung.

From the overlooking of this intuition proceeds all that has been said by philosophers and by men of science themselves about the "relativity" of scientific knowledge. *What is relative is the symbolic knowledge by pre-existing concepts, which proceeds from the fixed to the moving, and not the intuitive knowledge which installs itself in that which is moving and adopts the very life of things.* This intuition attains the absolute.

Science and metaphysics therefore come together in intuition. A truly intuitive philosophy would realize the much-desired union of science and metaphysics. While it would make of metaphysics a positive science—that is, a progressive and indefinitely perfectible one—it would at the same time lead the positive sciences, properly so-called, to become conscious of their true scope, often far greater than they imagine. It would put more science into metaphysics, and more metaphysics into science. It would result in restoring the continuity between the intuitions which the various sciences have obtained here and there in the course of their history, and which they have obtained only by strokes of genius.

IX. That there are not two different ways of knowing

---

[1] On this point as on several other questions treated in the present essay, see the interesting articles by MM. Le Roy, Vincent, and Wilbois, which have appeared in the *Revue de Métaphysique et de Morale*.

things fundamentally, that the various sciences have their root in metaphysics, is what the ancient philosophers generally thought. Their error did not lie there. It consisted in their being always dominated by the belief, so natural to the human mind, that a variation can only be the expression and development of what is invariable. Whence it followed that action was an enfeebled contemplation, duration a deceptive and shifting image of immobile eternity, the Soul a fall from the Idea. The whole of the philosophy which begins with Plato and culminates in Plotinus is the development of a principle which may be formulated thus: "There is more in the immutable than in the moving, and we pass from the stable to the unstable by a mere diminution." Now it is the contrary which is true.

Modern science dates from the day when mobility was set up as an independent reality. It dates from the day when Galileo, setting a ball rolling down an inclined plane, firmly resolved to study this movement from top to bottom for itself, in itself, instead of seeking its principle in the concepts of *high* and *low,* two immobilities by which Aristotle believed he could adequately explain the mobility. And this is not an isolated fact in the history of science. Several of the great discoveries, of those at least which have transformed the positive sciences or which have created new ones, have been so many soundings in the depths of pure duration. The more living the reality touched, the deeper was the sounding.

But the lead-line sunk to the sea bottom brings up a fluid mass which the sun's heat quickly dries into solid and discontinuous grains of sand. And the intuition of duration, when it is exposed to the rays of the understanding, in like manner quickly turns into fixed, distinct, and immobile concepts. In the living mobility of things the understanding is bent on marking real or virtual stations, it notes departures and arrivals; for this is all that concerns the thought of man in so far as it is simply human. It is more than human to grasp what is happening in the interval. But philosophy can only be an effort to transcend the human condition.

Men of science have fixed their attention mainly on the concepts with which they have marked out the pathway of intuition. The more they laid stress on these residual products, which have turned into symbols, the more they attributed a symbolic character to every kind of science. And the more they believed in the symbolic character of science, the more did they indeed make science symbolical. Gradually they have blotted out all difference, in positive science, between the natural and the artificial, between the data of immediate intuition, and the enormous work of analysis which the understanding pursues round intuition. Thus they have prepared the way for a doctrine which affirms the relativity of all our knowledge.

But metaphysics has also labored to the same end.

How could the masters of modern philosophy, who have been renovators of science as well as of metaphysics, have had no sense of the moving continuity of reality? How could they have abstained from placing themselves in what we call concrete duration? They have done so to a greater extent than they were aware; above all, much more than they said. If we endeavor to link together, by a continuous connection, the intuitions about which systems have become organized, we find, together with other convergent and divergent lines, one very determinate direction of thought and of feeling. What is this latent thought? How shall we express the feeling? To borrow once more the language of the Platonists, we will say—depriving the words of their psychological sense, and giving the name of Idea to a certain settling down into easy intelligibility, and that of Soul to a certain longing after the restlessness of life—that an invisible current causes modern philosophy to place the Soul above the Idea. It thus tends, like modern science, and even more so than modern science, to advance in an opposite direction to ancient thought.

But this metaphysics, like this science, has enfolded its deeper life in a rich tissue of symbols, forgetting something that, while science needs symbols for its analytical development, the main object of metaphysics is to do away with symbols. Here, again, the understanding has pursued its work of fixing, dividing, and reconstructing. It has pursued this, it is true, under a rather different form. Without insisting on a point which we propose to develop elsewhere, it is enough here to say that the understanding, whose function it is to operate on stable elements, may look for stability either in *relations* or in *things*. In so far as it works on concepts of relations, it culminates in *scientific* symbolism. In so far as it works on concepts of things, it culminates in *metaphysical* symbolism. But in both cases the arrangement comes from the understanding. Hence, it would fain believe itself independent. Rather than recognize at once what it owes to an intuition of the depths of reality, it prefers exposing itself to the danger that its whole work may be looked upon as nothing but an artificial arrangement of symbols. So that if we were to hold on to the letter of what metaphysicians and scientists say, and also to the material aspect of what they do, we might believe that the metaphysicians have dug a deep tunnel beneath reality, that the scientists have thrown an elegant bridge over it, but that the moving stream of things passes between these two artificial constructions without touching them. . . .

* * *

Modern science is neither one nor simple. It rests, I freely admit, on ideas which in the end we find clear; but these ideas have gradually become clear through the use made of them; they owe most of their clearness to the light which the facts, and the applications to which they led, have by reflection shed on them—the clearness of a concept being scarcely anything more at bottom than the certainty, at last obtained, of manipulating the concept profitably. At its origin, more than one of these concepts must have appeared obscure, not easily reconcilable with the concepts already admitted into science, and indeed very near the border-line of absurdity. This means that science does not proceed by an orderly dovetailing together of concepts predestined to fit each other exactly. True and fruitful ideas are so many close contacts with currents of reality, which do not necessarily converge on the same point. However, the concepts in which they lodge themselves manage somehow, by rubbing off each other's corners, to settle down well enough together.

On the other hand, modern metaphysics is not made up of solutions so radical that they can culminate in irreducible oppositions. It would be so, no doubt, if there were no means of accepting at the same time and on the same level the thesis and antithesis of the antinomies. But philosophy consists precisely in this, that by an effort of intuition one places oneself within that concrete reality, of which the *Critique* takes from without the two opposed views, thesis and antithesis. I could never imagine how black and white interpenetrate if I had never seen gray; but once I have seen gray I easily understand how it can be considered from two points of view, that of white and of black. Doctrines which have a certain basis of intuition escape the Kantian criticism exactly in so far as they are intuitive; and these doctrines are the whole of metaphsyics, provided we ignore the metaphysics which is fixed and dead in *theses,* and consider only that which is living in *philosophers.* The divergencies between the schools—that is, broadly speaking, between the groups of disciples formed round a few great masters—are certainly striking. But would we find them as marked between the masters themselves? Something here dominates the diversity of systems, something, we repeat, which is simple and definite like a sounding, about which one feels that it has touched at greater or less depth the bottom of the same ocean, though each time it brings up to the surface very different materials. It is on these materials that the disciples usually work; in this lies the function of analysis. And the master, in so far as he formulates, develops, and translates into abstract ideas what he brings, is already in a way his own disciple. But the simple act which started the analysis, and which conceals itself behind the analysis, proceeds from a faculty quite different from the analytical. This is, by its very definition, intuition.

In conclusion, we may remark that there is nothing mysterious in this faculty. Every one of us has had occasion to exercise it to a certain extent. Any one of us, for instance, who has attempted literary composition, knows that when the subject has been studied at length, the materials all collected, and the notes all made, something more is needed in order to set about the work of composition itself, and that is an often very painful effort to place ourselves directly at the heart of the subject, and to seek as deeply as possible an impulse, after which we need only let ourselves go. This impulse, once received, starts the mind on a path where it re-discovers all the information it had collected, and a thousand other details besides; it develops and analyzes itself into terms which could be enumerated indefinitely. The farther we go, the more terms we discover; we shall never say all that could be said, and yet, if we turn back suddenly upon the impulse that we feel behind us, and try to seize it, it is gone; for it was not a thing, but the direction of a movement, and though indefinitely extensible, it is infinitely simple. Metaphysical intuition seems to be something of the same kind. What corresponds here to the documents and notes of literary composition is the sum of observations and experience gathered together by positive science. For we do not obtain an intuition from reality—that is, an intellectual sympathy with the most intimate part of it—unless we have won its confidence by a long fellowship with its superficial manifestations. And it is not merely a question of assimilating the most conspicuous facts; so immense a mass of facts must be accumulated and fused together, that in this fusion all the preconceived and premature ideas which observers may unwittingly have put into their observations will be certain to neutralize each other. In this way only can the bare materiality of the known facts be exposed to view. Even in the simple and privileged case which we have used as an example, even for the direct contact of the self with the self, the final effort of distinct intuition would be impossible to any one who had not combined and compared with each other a very large number of psychological analyses. The masters of modern philosophy were men who had assimilated all the scientific knowledge of their time, and the partial eclipse of metaphysics for the last half-century has evidently no other cause than the extraordinary difficulty which the philosopher finds today in getting into touch with positive science, which has become far too specialized. But metaphysical intuition, although it can be obtained only through material knowledge, is quite other than the mere summary or synthesis of that knowledge. It is distinct from these, we repeat, as the motor impulse is distinct from the path traversed by the moving body, as the tension of the spring is distinct from the visible movements of the pendulum. In this sense metaphysics has nothing in common with a generalization of facts, and nevertheless it might be defined as *integral experience*.

TIME AND FREE WILL [1]

Authorized Translation by F. L. POGSON, M.A.

. . . conscious life displays two aspects according as we perceive it directly or by refraction through space. Considered in themselves, the deep-seated conscious states have no relation to quantity, they are pure quality; they intermingle in such a way that we cannot tell whether they are one or several, nor even examine them from this point of view without at once altering their nature. The duration which they thus create is a duration whose moments do not constitute a numerical multiplicity: to characterize these moments by saying that they encroach upon one another would still be to distinguish them. If each of us lived a purely individual life, if there were neither society nor language, would our consciousness grasp the series of inner states in this unbroken form? Undoubtedly it would not quite succeed, because we should still retain the idea of a homogeneous space in which objects are sharply distinguished from one another, and because it is too convenient to set out in such a medium the somewhat cloudy states which first attract the attention of consciousness, in order to resolve them into simpler terms. But mark that the intuition of a homogeneous

[1] Written from 1883 to 1887 and first published in 1889 as *Essai sur les données immédiates de la conscience*. These extracts from Henri Bergson, *Time and Free Will*, trans. by F. L. Pogson. By permission of The Macmillan Company, publishers. Copyright, 1910. Pp. 137–139, 230–232.

space is already a step towards social life. Probably animals do not picture to themselves, beside their sensations, as we do, an external world quite distinct from themselves, which is the common property of all conscious beings. Our tendency to form a clear picture of this externality of things and the homogeneity of their medium is the same as the impulse which leads us to live in common and to speak. But, in proportion as the conditions of social life are more completely realized, the current which carries our conscious states from within outwards is strengthened; little by little these states are made into objects or things; they break off not only from one another, but from ourselves. Henceforth we no longer perceive them except in the homogeneous medium in which we have set their image, and through the word which lends them its commonplace color. Thus a second self is formed which obscures the first, a self whose existence is made up of distinct moments, whose states are separated from one another and easily expressed in words. I do not mean, here, to split up the personality, nor to bring back in another form the numerical multiplicity which I shut out at the beginning. It it the same self which perceives distinct states at first, and which, by afterwards concentrating its attention, will see these states melt into one another like the crystals of a snowflake when touched for some time with the finger. And, in truth, for the sake of language, the self has everything to gain by not bringing back confusion where order reigns, and in not upsetting this ingenious arrangement of almost impersonal states by which it has ceased to form "a kingdom within a kingdom." An inner life with well distinguished moments and with clearly characterized states will answer better the requirements of social life. Indeed, a superficial psychology may be content with describing it without thereby falling into error, on condition, however, that it restricts itself to the study of what has taken place and leaves out what is going on. But if, passing from statics to dynamics, this psychology claims to reason about things in the making as it reasoned about things made, if it offers us the concrete and living self as an association of terms which are distinct from one another and are set side by side in a homogeneous medium, it will see difficulty after difficulty rising in its path. And these difficul ties will multiply the greater the efforts it makes to over- come them, for all its efforts will only bring into clearer light the absurdity of the fundamental hypothesis by which it spreads out time in space and puts succession at the very centre of simultaneity. We shall see that the contradictions implied in the problems of causality, freedom, personality, spring from no other source, and that, if we wish to get rid of them, we have only to go back to the real and concrete self and give up its symbolical substitute. . . .

The main object of science is to forecast and measure: now we cannot forecast physical phenomena except on condition that we assume that they do not *endure* as we do; and, on the other hand, the only thing we are able to measure is space. Hence the breach here comes about of itself between quality and quantity, between true duration and pure extensity. But when we turn to our conscious states, we have everything to gain by keeping up the illusion through which we make them share in the reciprocal externality of outer things, be- cause this distinctness, and at the same time this solidifica- tion, enables us to give them fixed names in spite of their instability, and distinct ones in spite of their interpenetration. It enables us to objectify them, to throw them out into the current of social life.

Hence there are finally two different selves, one of which is, as it were, the external projection of the other, its spatial and, so to speak, social representation. We reach the former by deep introspection, which leads us to grasp our inner states as living things, constantly *becoming,* as states not amenable to measure, which permeate one another and of which the succession in duration has nothing in common with juxtaposition in homogeneous space. But the moments at which we thus grasp ourselves are rare, and that is just why we are rarely free. The greater part of the time we live outside ourselves, hardly perceiving anything of ourselves but our own ghost, a colorless shadow which pure duration projects into homogeneous space. Hence our life unfolds in space rather than in time; we live for the external world rather than for ourselves; we speak rather than think; we "are acted" rather than act ourselves. To act freely is to recover possession of oneself, and to get back into pure duration.

MATTER AND MEMORY [1]

Authorized Translation by Nancy Margaret Paul and W. Scott Palmer

. . . Speaking generally, the psychical state seems to us to be, in most cases, immensely wider than the cerebral state. I mean that the brain state indicates only a very small part of the mental state, that part which is capable of translating itself into movements of locomotion. Take a complex thought which unrolls itself in a chain of abstract reasoning. This thought is accompanied by images, that are at least nascent. And these images themselves are not pictured in consciousness without some foreshadowing, in the form of a sketch or a tendency, of the movements by which these images would be acted or played in space,—would, that is to say, impress particular attitudes upon the body, and set free all that they implicitly contain of spatial movement. Now, of all the thought which is unrolling, this, in our view, is what the cerebral state indicates at every moment. He who could penetrate into the interior of a brain and see what happens there, would probably obtain full details of these sketched-out, or prepared, movements; there is no proof that he would learn

[1] First published in 1896, this translation is from the fifth French edition of 1908, with an introduction which supersedes that in the original edition. Selections are from Henri Bergson, *Matter and Memory*, trans. by Nancy Margaret Paul and W. Scott Palmer. By permission of The Macmillan Company, publishers. Copyright, 1911. Pp. xiii–xvii, 19–20, 23, 40–41, 69–72, 74–75, 78–81, 92–95, 122–123, 128–130, 180–182, 193–194.

anything else. Were he endowed with a superhuman intellect, did he possess the key to psycho-physiology, he would know no more of what is going on in the corresponding consciousness than we should know of a play from the comings and goings of the actors upon the stage.

That is to say, the relation of the mental to the cerebral is not a constant, any more than it is a simple, relation. According to the nature of the play that is being acted, the movements of the players tell us more or less about it: nearly everything, if it is a pantomime; next to nothing, if it is a delicate comedy. Thus our cerebral state contains more or less of our mental state in the measure that we reel off our psychic life into action or wind it up into pure knowledge.

There are then, in short, divers *tones* of mental life, or, in other words, our psychic life may be lived at different heights, now nearer to action, now further removed from it, according to the degree of our *attention to life*. Here we have one of the ruling ideas of this book—the idea, indeed which served as the starting-point of our inquiry. That which is usually held to be a greater complexity of the psychical state appears to us, from our point of view, to be a greater dilation of the whole personality, which, normally narrowed down by action, expands with the unscrewing of the vice in which it has allowed itself to be squeezed, and, always whole and undivided, spreads itself over a wider and wider surface. That which is commonly held to be a disturbance of the psychic life itself, an inward disorder, a disease of the personality, appears to us, from our point of view, to be an unloosing or a breaking of the tie which binds this psychic life to its motor accompaniment, a weakening or an impairing of our attention to outward life. . . .

*
* *

. . . we believe that the reader will find his way if he keeps a fast hold on the two principles which we have used as a clue throughout our own researches. The first is that in psychological analysis we must never forget the utilitarian character of our mental functions, which are essentially turned towards action. The second is that the habits formed in action find their way up to the sphere of speculation, where they create fictitious problems, and that metaphysics must begin by dispersing this artificial obscurity.

THE CHOICE OF IMAGES

. . . In our opinion, then, the brain is no more than a kind of central telephonic exchange: its office is to allow communication, or to delay it. It adds nothing to what it receives; but, as all the organs of perception send to it their ultimate prolongations, and as all the motor mechanisms of the spinal cord and of the medulla oblongata have in it their accredited representatives, it really constitutes a centre, where the peripheral excitation gets into relation with this or that motor mechanism, chosen and no longer prescribed. On the other hand, as a great multitude of motor tracks can open simultaneously in this substance to one and the same excitation from the periphery, this disturbance may subdivide to any extent, and consequently dissipate itself in innumerable motor reactions which are merely nascent. Hence the office of the brain is sometimes to conduct the movement received to a *chosen* organ of reaction, and sometimes to open this movement the *totality* of the motor tracks, so that it may manifest there all the potential reactions with which it is charged, and may divide and so disperse. In other words, the brain appears to us to be an instrument of analysis in regard to the movement received, and an instrument of selection in regard to the movement executed. But, in the one case as in the other, its office is limited to the transmission and division of movement. And no more in the higher centres of the cortex than in the spinal cord do the nervous elements work with a view to knowledge: they do but indicate a number of possible actions at once, or organize one of them. . . .

The degree of independence of which a living being is master, or, as we shall say, the zone of indetermination which surrounds its activity, allows, then, of an *a priori* estimate of the number and the distance of the things with which it is in relation. Whatever this relation may be, whatever be the inner nature of perception, we can affirm that its amplitude gives the exact measure of the indetermination of the act which is to follow. So that we can formulate this law: *perception is master of space in the exact measure in which action is master of time.* . . .

. . . We are too much inclined to regard the living body as a world within a world, the nervous system as a separate being, of which the function is, first, to elaborate perceptions, and then to create movements. The truth is that my nervous system, interposed between the objects which affect my body and those which I can influence, is a mere conductor, transmitting, sending back, or inhibiting movement. This conductor is composed of an enormous number of threads which stretch from the periphery to the centre, and from the centre to the periphery. As many threads as pass from the periphery to the centre, so many points of space are there able to make an appeal to my will and put, so to speak, an elementary question to my motor activity. Every such question is what is termed a perception. Thus perception is diminished by one of its elements each time one of the threads termed sensory is cut, because some part of the external object then becomes unable to appeal to activity; and it is also diminished whenever a stable habit has been formed, because this time the ready-made response renders the question unnecessary. What disappears in either case is the apparent reflection of the stimulus upon itself, the return of the light on the image whence it comes; or rather that dissociation, that *discernment,* whereby the perception is disengaged from the image. We may therefore say that while the detail of perception is moulded exactly upon that of the nerves termed sensory, perception as a whole has its true and final explanation in the tendency of the body to movement. . . .

PURE PERCEPTION

If we went no further (than the theory of *pure* perception), the part of consciousness in perception would thus be confined to the threading on the continuous string of memory an uninterrupted series of instantaneous visions, which would be a part of things rather than of ourselves. That this *is* the chief office of consciousness in external perception is indeed what we may deduce *a priori* from the very definition of living bodies. For though the function of these bodies is to receive stimulations in order to elaborate them into unforeseen reactions, still the choice of the reaction cannot be the work of chance. This choice is likely to be inspired by past experience, and the reaction does not take place without an appeal to the memories which analogous situations may have left behind them. The indetermination of acts to be accomplished requires then, if it is not to be confounded with pure caprice, the preservation of the images perceived. It may be said that we have no grasp of the future without an equal and corresponding outlook over the past, that the onrush of our activity makes a void behind it into which memories flow, and that memory is thus the reverberation, in the sphere of conscious-

ness, of the indetermination of our will.—But the action of
memory goes further and deeper than this superficial glance
would suggest. The moment has come to reinstate memory
in perception, to correct in this way the element of exaggera-
tion in our conclusions, and so to determine with more precision the point of contact between consciousness and things,
between the body and the spirit.

We assert, at the outset, that if there be memory, that is,
the survival of past images, these images must constantly
mingle with our perception of the present, and may even take
its place. For if they have survived it is with a view to utility;
at every moment they complete our present experience, enriching it with experience already acquired; and, as the latter
is ever increasing, it must end by covering up and submerg-
ing the former. It is indisputable that the basis of real, and so
to speak instantaneous, intuition, on which our perception
of the external world is developed, is a small matter compared with all that memory adds to it. Just because the
recollection of earlier analogous intuitions is more useful
than intuition itself, being bound up in memory with the
whole series of subsequent events, and capable thereby of
throwing a better light on our decision, it supplants the
real intuition of which the office is then merely—we shall
prove it later—to call up the recollection, to give it a body,
to render it active and thereby actual. We had every right,
then, to say that the coincidence of perception with the
object perceived exists in theory rather than in fact. We must
take into account that perception ends by being merely an
occasion for remembering, that we measure in practice the
degree of reality by the degree of utility, and, finally, that it is
our interest to regard as mere signs of the real those immediate intuitions which are, in fact, part and parcel with reality.
But here we discover the mistake of those who say that to

perceive is to project externally unextended sensations which have been drawn from our own depths, and then to develop them in space. They have no difficulty in showing that our *complete* perception is filled with images which belong to us personally, with exteriorized (that is to say recollected) images; but they forget that an impersonal basis remains in which perception coincides with the object perceived; and which is, in fact, externality itself.

The capital error, the error which, passing over from psychology into metaphysic, shuts us out in the end from the knowledge both of body and of spirit, is that which sees only a difference of intensity, instead of a difference of nature, between pure perception and memory. Our perceptions are undoubtedly interlaced with memories, and inversely, a memory, as we shall show later, only becomes actual by borrowing the body of some perception into which it slips. These two acts, perception and recollection, always interpenetrate each other, are always exchanging something of their substance as by a process of endosmosis. . . .

THE PROBLEM OF MATTER

Restore, on the contrary, the true character of perception; recognize in pure perception a system of nascent acts which plunges roots deep into the real; and at once perception is seen to be radically distinct from recollection; the reality of things is no more constructed or reconstructed, but touched, penetrated, lived; and the problem at issue between realism and idealism, instead of giving rise to interminable metaphysical discussions, is solved, or rather dissolved by intuition. . . .

For it is possible to sum up our conclusions as to pure perception by saying that *there is in matter something more than, but not something different from, that which is actually given.* Undoubtedly conscious perception does not compass the whole of matter, since it consists, in so far as it is conscious, in the separation, or the "discernment," of that which, in matter, interests our various needs. But between this perception of matter and matter itself there is but a difference of degree and not of kind, pure perception standing towards matter in the relation of part to whole. This amounts to saying that matter cannot exercise powers of any kind other than those which we perceive. It has no mysterious virtue, it can conceal none. To take a definite example, one moreover which interests us most nearly, we may say that the nervous system, a material mass presenting certain qualities of color, resistance, cohesion, and so on, may well possess unperceived physical properties, but physical properties only. And hence it can have no other office than to receive, inhibit, or transmit movement. . . .

The truth is that there is one, and only one, method of refuting materialism: it is to show that matter is precisely that which it appears to be. Thereby we eliminate all virtuality, all hidden power from matter, and establish the phenomena of spirit as an independent reality. But to do this we must leave to matter those qualities which materialists and spiritualists alike strip from it: the latter that they may make of them representations of the spirit, the former that they may regard them only as the accidental garb of space.

This, indeed, is the attitude of common sense with regard to matter, and for this reason common sense believes in spirit. It seems to us that philosophy should here adopt the attitude of common sense, although correcting it in one respect. Memory, inseparable in practice from perception, imports the past into the present, contracts into a single intuition many moments of duration, and thus by a twofold operation compels us, *de facto,* to perceive matter in ourselves, whereas we, *de jure,* perceive matter within matter.

Hence the capital importance of the problem of memory. If it is memory above all that lends to perception its subjective character, the philosophy of matter must aim in the first instance, we said, at eliminating the contributions of memory. We must now add that, as pure perception gives us the whole or at least the essential part of matter (since the rest comes from memory and is superadded to matter), it follows that memory must be, in principle, a power absolutely independent of matter. If, then, spirit is a reality, it is here, in the phenomenon of memory, that we may come into touch with it experimentally. . . .

THE TWO FORMS OF MEMORY

Following to the end this fundamental distinction (between memory on first reading and memorizing by rote), we are confronted by two different memories theoretically independent. The first records, in the form of memory-images, all the events of our daily life as they occur in time; it neglects no detail; it leaves to each fact, to each gesture, its place and date. Regardless of utility or of practical application, it stores up the past by the mere necessity of its own nature. By this memory is made possible the intelligent, or rather intellectual, recognition of a perception already experienced; in it we take refuge every time that, in the search for a particular image, we remount the slope of our past. But every perception is prolonged into a nascent action; and while the images are taking their place and order in this memory, the movements which continue them modify the organism, and create in the body new dispositions towards action. Thus is gradually formed an experience of an entirely different order, which accumulates within the body, a series of mechanisms wound up and ready, with reactions to external stimuli ever more numerous and more varied, and answers ready prepared to an ever-growing number of possible solicitations. We become conscious of these mechanisms as they come into play; and this consciousness of a whole past of efforts stored up in the present is indeed also a memory, but a memory profoundly different from the first, always bent upon action, seated in the present and looking only to the future. It has retained from the past only the intelligently coördinated movements which represent the accumulated efforts of the past; and it recovers those past efforts, not in the memory-images which recall them, but in the definite order and systematic character with which the actual movements take place. In truth, it no longer *represents* our past to us, it *acts* it; and if it still deserves the name of memory, it is not because it conserves bygone images, but because it prolongs their useful effect into the present moment. . . .

When psychologists talk of recollection as of a fold in a material, as of an impress graven deeper by repetition, they forget that the immense majority of our memories bear upon events and details of our life of which the essence is to have a date, and consequently to be incapable of being repeated. The memories which we acquire voluntarily by repetition are rare and exceptional. On the contrary, the recording, by memory, of facts and images unique in their kind takes place at every moment of duration. But inasmuch as *learnt* memories are more useful, they are more remarked. And as the acquisition of these memories by a repetition of the same effort resembles the well-known process of habit, we prefer to set this kind of memory in the foreground, to erect it into the model memory, and to see in spontaneous recollection only the same phenomenon in a nascent state, the be-

ginning of a lesson learnt by heart. But how can we over-
look the radical difference between that which must be built
up by repetition and that which is essentially incapable of
being repeated? Spontaneous recollection is perfect from the
outset; time can add nothing to its image without disfiguring
it; it retains in memory its place and date. On the contrary,
a learnt recollection passes out of time in the measure that
the lesson is better known; it becomes more and more impersonal, more and more foreign to our past life. Repetition,
therefore, in no sense effects the conversion of the first into
the last; its office is merely to utilize more and more the movements by which the first was continued, in order to organize
them together and, by setting up a mechanism, to create a
bodily habit. Indeed, this habit could not be called a remem-
brance, were it not that I remember that I have acquired it;
and I remember its acquisition only because I appeal to that
memory which is spontaneous, which dates events and records them but once. Of the two memories, then, which
we have just distinguished, the first appears to be memory
par excellence. The second, that generally studied by psychologists, is *habit interpreted by memory* rather than memory itself. . . .

RECOLLECTIONS AND MOVEMENTS

While external perception provokes on our part movements which retrace its main lines, our memory directs upon
the perception received the memory-images which resemble
it and which are already sketched out by the movements
themselves. Memory thus creates anew the present perception; or rather it doubles this perception by reflecting upon it
either its own image or some other memory-image of the
same kind. If the retained or remembered image will not
cover all the details of the image that is being perceived, an

appeal is made to the deeper and more distant regions of memory, until other details that are already known come to project themselves upon those details that remain unperceived. And the operation may go on indefinitely;—memory strengthening and enriching perception, which, in its turn becoming wider, draws into itself a growing number of complementary recollections. So let us no longer think of a mind which disposes of some fixed quantity of light, now diffusing it around, now concentrating it on a single point. Metaphor for metaphor, we would rather compare the elementary work of attention to that of the telegraph clerk who, on receipt of an important despatch, sends it back again, word for word, in order to check its accuracy. . . .

The same psychical life, therefore, must be supposed to be repeated an endless number of times on the different storeys of memory, and the same act of the mind may be performed at varying heights. In the effort of attention, the mind is always concerned in its entirety, but it simplifies or complicates itself according to the level on which it chooses to to work. Usually it is the present perception which determines the direction of our mind; but, according to the degree of tension which our mind adopts and the height at which it takes its stand, the perception develops a greater or smaller number of images.

In other words, personal recollections, exactly localized, the series of which represents the course of our past experience, make up, all together, the last and largest enclosure of our memory. Essentially fugitive, they become materialized only by chance, either when an accidentally precise determination of our bodily attitude attracts them, or when the very indetermination of that attitude leaves a clear field to the caprices of their manifestations. But this outermost envelope contracts and repeats itself in inner and concentric circles, which in their narrower range enclose the same recollections grown smaller, more and more removed from their personal and original form, and more and more capable, from their lack of distinguishing features, of being applied to the present perception and of determining it after the manner of a species which defines and absorbs the individual. There comes a moment when the recollection thus brought down is capable of blending so well with the present perception that we cannot say where the perception ends or where memory begins. At that precise moment, memory, instead of capriciously sending in and calling back its images, follows regularly, in all their details, the movements of the body. . . .

THE UNCONSCIOUS

That which I call my present is my attitude with regard to the immediate future; it is my impending action. My present is, then, sensori-motor. Of my past, that alone becomes image and consequently sensation, at least nascent, which can collaborate in that action, insert itself in that attitude, in a word make itself useful; but, from the moment that it becomes image, the past leaves the state of pure memory and coincides with a certain part of my present. Memory actualized in an image differs, then, profoundly from pure memory. The image is a present state, and its sole share in the past is the memory whence it arose. Memory, on the contrary, powerless as long as it remains without utility, is pure from all admixture of sensation, is without attachment to the present, and is consequently unextended.

This radical powerlessness of pure memory is just what will enable us to understand how it is preserved in a latent state. Without as yet going to the heart of the matter, we will confine ourselves to the remark that our unwillingness to conceive *unconscious psychical states* is due, above all, to the fact that we hold consciousness to be the essential property of psychical states: so that a psychical state cannot, it seems, cease to be conscious without ceasing to exist. But if consciousness is but the characteristic note of the *present,* that is to say of the actually lived, in short of the *active,* then that which does not act may cease to belong to consciousness without therefore ceasing to exist in some manner. In other words, in the psychological domain, consciousness may not be the synonym of existence, but only of real action or of immediate efficacy; and, limiting thus the meaning of the term, we shall have less difficulty in representing to ourselves a psychical state which is unconscious, that is to say, ineffective. Whatever idea we may frame of consciousness in itself, such as it would be if it could work untrammeled, we cannot deny that, in a being which has bodily functions, the chief office of consciousness is to preside over action and to enlighten choice. Therefore it throws light on the immediate antecedents of the decision, and on those past recollections which can usefully combine with it; all else remains in shadow. . . .

RELATION OF PAST AND PRESENT

But how can the past, which, by hypothesis, has ceased to be, preserve itself? Have we not here a real contradiction?—We reply that the question is just whether the past has ceased to exist or whether it has simply ceased to be useful. You define the present in an arbitrary manner as *that which is,* whereas the present is simply *what is being made.* Nothing *is* less than the present moment, if you understand by that the indivisible limit which divides the past from the future. When we think this present as going to be, it exists not yet; and when we think it as existing, it is already past. If, on the other hand, what you are considering is the concrete present such as it is actually lived by consciousness, we may say that this present consists, in large measure, in the immediate past. In the fraction of a second which covers the briefest possible perception of light, billions of vibrations have taken place, of which the first is separated from the last by an interval which is enormously divided. Your perception, however instantaneous, consists then in an incalculable multitude of remembered elements; and in truth every perception is already memory. *Practically we perceive only the past,* the pure present being the invisible progress of the past gnawing into the future.

Consciousness, then, illumines, at each moment of time, that immediate part of the past which, impending over the future, seeks to realize and to associate with it. Solely preoccupied in thus determining an undetermined future, consciousness may shed a little of its light on those of our states, more remote in the past, which can be usefully combined with our present state, that is to say, with our immediate past: the rest remains in the dark. It is in this illuminated part of our history that we remain seated, in virtue of the fundamental law of life, which is a law of action: hence the difficulty we experience in conceiving memories which are preserved in the shadow. Our reluctance to admit the integral survival of the past has its origin, then, in the very bent of our psychical life,—an unfolding of states wherein our interest prompts us to look at that which is unrolling, and not at that which is entirely unrolled. . . .

CREATIVE EVOLUTION [1]

Authorized Translation by ARTHUR MITCHELL

DURATION

The existence of which we are most assured and which we know best is unquestionably our own, for of every other object we have notions which may be considered external and superficial, whereas, of ourselves, our perception is internal and profound. What, then, do we find? In this privileged case, what is the precise meaning of the word "exist"? Let us recall here briefly the conclusions of an earlier work.

I find, first of all, that I pass from state to state. I am warm or cold, I am merry or sad, I work or I do nothing, I look at what is around me or I think of something else. Sensations, feelings, volitions, ideas—such are the changes into which my existence is divided and which color it in turns. I change, then, without ceasing. But this is not saying enough. Change is far more radical than we are at first inclined to suppose.

For I speak of each of my states as if it formed a block and were a separate whole. I say indeed that I change, but the change seems to me to reside in the passage from one state to the next: of each state, taken separately, I am apt to think that it remains the same during all the time that it prevails.

[1] *L'Évolution Créatrice* was first published in 1907. These selections are from Henri Bergson, *Creative Evolution,* trans. by Arthur Mitchell. Copyright, 1911 by Henry Holt and Company, Inc. Copyright, 1938, by Arthur Mitchell. Pp. 1–7, 48–50, 53–55, 87–90, 98–105, 134–143, 163–165, 218–224, 247–251, 263–266, and 267–271.

Nevertheless, a slight effort of attention would reveal to me
that there is no feeling, no idea, no volition which is not
undergoing change every moment: if a mental state ceased
to vary, its duration would cease to flow. Let us take the most
stable of internal states, the visual perception of a motionless
external object. The object may remain the same, I may look
at it from the same side, at the same angle, in the same light;
nevertheless the vision I now have of it differs from that
which I have just had, even if only because the one is an
instant older than the other. My memory is there, which
conveys something of the past into the present. My mental
state, as it advances on the road of time, is continually swell-
ing with the duration which it accumulates: it goes on increasing—rolling upon itself, as a snowball on the snow.
Still more is this the case with states more deeply internal,
such as sensations, feelings, desires, and so on, which do not
correspond, like a simple visual perception, to an unvarying
external object. But it is expedient to disregard this uninterrupted change, and to notice it only when it becomes sufficient to impress a new attitude on the body, a new direction
on the attention. Then, and then only, we find that our state
has changed. The truth is that we change without ceasing,
and that the state itself is nothing but change.

This amounts to saying that there is no essential difference
between passing from one state to another and persisting in
the same state. If the state which "remains the same" is more
varied than we think, on the other hand, the passing from
one state to another resembles, more than we imagine, a
single state being prolonged; the transition is continuous.
But, just because we close our eyes to the unceasing variation
of every psychical state, we are obliged, when the change has
become so considerable as to force itself on our attention, to
speak as if a new state were placed alongside the previous

one. Of this new state we assume that it remains unvarying in its turn, and so on endlessly. The apparent discontinuity of the psychical life is then due to our attention being fixed on it by a series of separate acts: actually there is only a gentle slope; but in following the broken line of our acts of attention, we think we perceive separate steps. True, our psychic life is full of the unforeseen. A thousand incidents arise, which seem to be cut off from those which precede them, and to be disconnected from those which follow. Discontinuous though they appear, however, in point of fact they stand out against the continuity of a background on which they are designed, and to which indeed they owe the intervals that separate them; they are the beats of the drum which break forth here and there in the symphony. Our attention fixes on them because they interest it more, but each of them is borne by the fluid mass of our whole psychical existence. Each is only the best illuminated point of a moving zone which comprises all that we feel or think or will—all, in short, that we are at any given moment. It is this entire zone which in reality makes up our state. Now, states thus defined cannot be regarded as distinct elements. They continue each other in an endless flow.

But, as our attention has distinguished and separated them artificially, it is obliged next to reunite them by an artificial bond. It imagines, therefore, a formless *ego,* indifferent and unchangeable, on which it threads the psychic states which it has set up as independent entities. Instead of a flux of fleeting shades merging into each other, it perceives distinct and, so to speak, *solid* colors, set side by side like the beads of a necklace; it must perforce then suppose a thread, also itself solid, to hold the beads together. But if this colorless substratum is perpetually colored by that which covers it, it is for us, in its indeterminateness, as if it did not exist, since we only perceive what is colored, or, in other words, psychic states. As a matter of fact, this substratum has no reality; it is merely a symbol intended to recall unceasingly to our consciousness the artificial character of the process by which the attention places clean-cut states side by side, where actually there is a continuity which unfolds. If our existence were composed of separate states with an impassive ego to unite them, for us there would be no duration. For an ego which does not change does not *endure,* and a psychic state which remains the same so long as it is not replaced by the following state does not *endure* either. Vain, therefore, is the attempt to range such states beside each other on the ego supposed to sustain them: never can these solids strung upon a solid make up that duration which flows. What we actually obtain in this way is an artificial imitation of the internal life, a static equivalent which will lend itself better to the requirements of logic and language, just because we have eliminated from it the element of real time. But, as regards the psychical life unfolding beneath the symbols which conceal it, we readily perceive that time is just the stuff it is made of.

There is, moreover, no stuff more resistant nor more substantial. For our duration is not merely one instant replacing another; if it were, there would never be anything but the present—no prolonging of the past into the actual, no evolution, no concrete duration. Duration is the continuous progress of the past which gnaws into the future and which swells as it advances. And as the past grows without ceasing, so also there is no limit to its preservation. Memory, as we have tried to prove,[1] is not a faculty of putting away recollections in a drawer, or of inscribing them in a register. There is no register, no drawer; there is not even, properly speaking, a faculty, for a faculty works intermittently, when it will or

---

[1] *Matière et mémoire* (Paris, 1896), chaps. ii and iii.

when it can, whilst the piling up of the past upon the past goes on without relaxation. In reality, the past is preserved by itself, automatically. In its entirety, probably, it follows us at every instant; all that we have felt, thought and willed from our earliest infancy is there, leaning over the present which is about to join it, pressing against the portals of consciousness that would fain leave it outside. The cerebral mechanism is arranged just so as to drive back into the unconscious almost the whole of this past, and to admit beyond the threshold only that which can cast light on the present situation or further the action now being prepared—in short, only that which can give *useful* work. At the most, a few superfluous recollections may succeed in smuggling themselves through the half-open door. These memories, messengers from the unconscious, remind us of what we are dragging behind us unawares. But, even though we may have no distinct idea of it, we feel vaguely that our past remains present to us. What are we, in fact, what is our *character,* if not the condensation of the history that we have lived from our birth—nay, even before our birth, since we bring with us prenatal dispositions? Doubtless we think with only a small part of our past, but it is with our entire past, including the original bent of our soul, that we desire, will and act. Our past, then, as a whole, is made manifest to us in its impulse; it is felt in the form of tendency, although a small part of it only is known in the form of idea.

From this survival of the past it follows that consciousness cannot go through the same state twice. The circumstances may still be the same, but they will act no longer on the same person, since they find him at a new moment of his history. Our personality, which is being built up each instant with its accumulated experience, changes without ceasing. By changing, it prevents any state, although superficially identical with another, from ever repeating it in its very depth. That is why our duration is irreversible. We could not live over again a single moment, for we should have to begin by effacing the memory of all that had followed. Even could we erase this memory from our intellect, we could not from our will.

Thus our personality shoots, grows and ripens without ceasing. Each of its moments is something new added to what was before. We may go further: it is not only something new, but something unforeseeable. Doubtless, my present state is explained by what was in me and by what was acting on me a moment ago. In analyzing it I should find no other elements. But even a superhuman intelligence would not have been able to foresee the simple indivisible form which gives to these purely abstract elements their concrete organization. For to foresee consists of projecting into the future what has been perceived in the past, or of imagining for a later time a new grouping, in a new order, of elements already perceived. But that which has never been perceived, and which is at the same time simple, is necessarily unforeseeable. Now such is the case with each of our states, regarded as a moment in a history that is gradually unfolding: it is simple, and it cannot have been already perceived, since it concentrates in its indivisibility all that has been perceived and what the present is adding to it besides. It is an original moment of a no less original history.

The finished portrait is explained by the features of the model, by the nature of the artist, by the colors spread out on the palette; but, even with the knowledge of what explains it, no one, not even the artist, could have foreseen exactly what the portrait would be, for to predict it would have been to produce it before it was produced—an absurd hypothesis which is its own refutation. Even so with regard to the moments of our life, of which we are the artisans. Each of them is a kind of creation. And just as the talent of the painter is formed or deformed—in any case, is modified—under the very influence of the works he produces, so each of our states, at the moment of its issue, modifies our personality, being indeed the new form that we are just assuming. It is then right to say that what we do depends on what we are; but it is necessary to add also that we are, to a certain extent, what we do, and that we are creating ourselves continually. This creation of self by self is the more complete, the more one reasons on what one does. For reason does not proceed in such matters as in geometry, where impersonal premises are given once for all, and an impersonal conclusion must perforce be drawn. Here, on the contrary, the same reasons may dictate to different persons, or to the same person at different moments, acts profoundly different, although equally reasonable. The truth is that they are not quite the same reasons, since they are not those of the same person, nor of the same moment. That is why we cannot deal with them in the abstract, from outside, as in geometry, nor solve for another the problems by which he is faced in life. Each must solve them from within, on his own account. But we need not go more deeply into this. We are seeking only the precise meaning that our consciousness gives to this word "exist," and we find that, for a conscious being, to exist is to change, to change is to mature, to mature is to go on creating oneself endlessly. . . .

BIOLOGY AND PHILOSOPHY

Our reason, incorrigibly presumptuous, imagines itself possessed, by right of birth or by right of conquest, innate or acquired, of all the essential elements of the knowledge of truth. Even where it confesses that it does not know the object presented to it, it believes that its ignorance consists only in not knowing which one of its time-honored categories suits the new object. In what drawer, ready to open, shall we put it? In what garment, already cut out, shall we clothe it? Is it this, or that, or the other thing? And "this," and "that," and "the other thing" are always something already conceived, already known. The idea that for a new object we might have to create a new concept, perhaps a new method of thinking, is deeply repugnant to us. The history of philosophy is there, however, and shows us the eternal conflict of systems, the impossibility of satisfactorily getting the real into the ready-made garments of our ready-made concepts, the necessity of making to measure. But, rather than go to this extremity, our reason prefers to announce once for all, with a proud modesty, that it has to do only with the relative, and that the absolute is not in its province. This preliminary declaration enables it to apply its habitual method of thought without any scruple, and thus, under pretense that it does not touch the absolute, to make absolute judgments upon everything. Plato was the first to set up the theory that to know the real consists in finding its Idea, that is to say, in forcing it into a pre-existing frame already at our disposal—as if we implicitly possessed universal knowledge. But this belief is natural to the human intellect, always engaged as it is in determining under what former heading it shall catalogue any new object; and it may be said that, in a certain sense, we are all born Platonists.

Nowhere is the inadequacy of this method so obvious as in theories of life. If, in evolving in the direction of the vertebrates in general, of man and intellect in particular, life has had to abandon by the way many elements incompatible with this particular mode of organization and consign them, as we shall show, to other lines of development, it is the totality of these elements that we must find again and rejoin to the intellect proper, in order to grasp the true nature of vital activity. And we shall probably be aided in this by the fringe of vague intuition that surrounds our distinct—that is, intellectual—representation. For what can this useless fringe be, if not that part of the evolving principle which has not shrunk to the peculiar form of our organization, but has settled around it unasked for, unwanted? It is there, accordingly, that we must look for hints to expand the intellectual form of our thought; from there shall we derive the impetus necessary to lift us above ourselves. To form an idea of the whole of life cannot consist in combining simple ideas that have been left behind in us by life itself in the course of its evolution. How could the part be equivalent to the whole, the content to the container, a by-product of the vital operation to the operation itself? Such, however, is our illusion when we define the evolution of life as a "passage from the homogeneous to the heterogeneous," or by any other concept obtained by putting fragments of intellect side by side. We place ourselves in one of the points where evolution comes to a head—the principal one, no doubt, but not the only one; and there we do not even take all we find, for of the intellect we keep only one or two of the concepts by which it expresses itself; and it is this part of a part that we declare representative of the whole, of something indeed which goes beyond the concrete whole, I mean of the evolution movement of which this "whole" is only the present stage! The truth is, that to represent this the entire intellect would not be too much—nay, it would not be enough. It would be necessary to add to it what we find in every other terminal point of evolution. And these diverse and divergent elements must be considered as so many extracts which are, or at least which were, in their humblest form, mutually complementary. Only then might we have an inkling of the real nature of the evolution movement; and even then we should fail to grasp it completely, for we should still be dealing only with the evolved, which is a result, and not with evolution itself, which is the act by which the result is obtained. . . .

Let us indicate at once the principle of our demonstration. We said of life that, from its origin, it is the continuation of one and the same impetus, divided into divergent lines of evolution. Something has grown, something has developed by a series of additions which have been so many creations. This very development has brought about a dissociation of tendencies which were unable to grow beyond a certain point without becoming mutually incompatible. Strictly speaking, there is nothing to prevent our imagining that the evolution of life might have taken place in one single individual by means of a series of transformations spread over thousands of ages. Or, instead of a single individual, any number might be supposed, succeeding each other in a unilinear series. In both cases evolution would have had, so to speak, one dimension only. But evolution has actually taken place through millions of individuals, on divergent lines, each ending at a crossing from which new paths radiate, and so on indefinitely. If our hypothesis is justified, if the essential causes working along these diverse roads are of psychological nature, they must keep something in common in spite of the divergence of their effects, as school-fellows long separated keep the same memories of boyhood. Roads may fork or by-ways be opened along which dissociated elements may evolve in an independent manner, but nevertheless it is in virtue of the primitive impetus of the whole that the movement of the parts continues. Something of the whole, therefore, must abide in the parts; and this common element will be evident to us in some way, perhaps by the presence of identical organs in very different organisms. Suppose, for an instant, that the mechanistic explanation is the true one: evolution must then have occurred through a series of accidents added to one another, each new accident being preserved by selection if it is advantageous to that sum of former advantageous accidents which the present form of the living being represents. What likelihood is there that, by two entirely different series of accidents being added together, two entirely different evolutions will arrive at similar results? The more two lines of evolution diverge, the less probability is there that accidental outer influences or accidental inner variations bring about the construction of the same apparatus upon them, especially if there was no trace of this apparatus at the moment of divergence. But such similarity of the two products would be natural, on the contrary, in a hypothesis like ours: even in the latest channel there would be something of the impulsion received at the source. *Pure mechanism, then, would be refutable, and finality, in the special sense in which we understand it, would be demonstrable in a certain aspect, if it could be proved that life may manufacture the like apparatus, by unlike means, on divergent lines of evolution; and the strength of the proof would be proportional both to the divergency between the lines of evolution thus chosen and to the complexity of the similar structures found in them.* . . .

ÉLAN VITAL or *Vital Impetus*

So we come back, by a somewhat roundabout way, to the idea we started from, that of an *original impetus* of life, passing from one generation of germs to the following generation of germs through the developed organisms which bridge the interval between the generations. This impetus, sustained right along the lines of evolution among which it gets divided, is the fundamental cause of variations, at least of those that are regularly passed on, that accumulate and create new species. In general, when species have begun to diverge from a common stock, they accentuate their divergence as they progress in their evolution. Yet, in certain definite points they may evolve identically; in fact, they must do so if the hypothesis of a common impetus be accepted. This is just what we shall have to show now in a more precise way, by the same example we have chosen, the formation of the eye in mollusks and vertebrates. The idea of an "original impetus," moreover, will thus be made clearer.

Two points are equally striking in an organ like the eye: the complexity of its structure and the simplicity of its function. The eye is composed of distinct parts, such as the sclerotic, the cornea, the retina, the crystalline lens, and so on. In each of these parts the detail is infinite. The retina alone comprises three layers of nervous elements—multipolar cells, bipolar cells, visual cells—each of which has its individuality and is undoubtedly a very complicated organism: so complicated, indeed, is the retinal membrane in its intimate structure, that no simple description can give an adequate idea of it. The mechanism of the eye is, in short, composed of an infinity of mechanisms, all of extreme complexity. Yet vision is one simple fact. As soon as the eye opens, the visual act is effected. Just because the act is simple, the slightest negligence on the part of nature in the building of the infinitely complex machine would have made vision impossible. This contrast between the complexity of the organ and the unity of the function is what gives us pause.

A mechanistic theory is one which means to show us the gradual building-up of the machine under the influence of external circumstances intervening either directly by action on the tissues or indirectly by the selection of better-adapted ones. But, whatever form this theory may take, supposing it avails at all to explain the detail of the parts, it throws no light on their correlation.

Then comes the doctrine of finality, which says that the parts have been brought together on a preconceived plan with a view to a certain end. In this it likens the labor of nature to that of the workman, who also proceeds by the assemblage of parts with a view to the realization of an idea or the imitation of a model. Mechanism, here, reproaches finalism with its anthropomorphic character, and rightly. But it fails to see that itself proceeds according to this method —somewhat mutilated! True, it has got rid of the end pursued or the ideal model. But it also holds that nature has worked like a human being by bringing parts together, while a mere glance at the development of an embryo shows that life goes to work in a very different way. *Life does not proceed by the association and addition of elements, but by dissociation and division.*

We must get beyond both points of view, both mechanism and finalism being, at bottom, only standpoints to which the human mind has been led by considering the work of man. But in what direction can we go beyond them? We have said that in analyzing the structure of an organ, we can go on decomposing forever, although the function of the whole is a simple thing. This contrast between the infinite complexity of the organ and the extreme simplicity of the function is what should open our eyes.

In general, when the same object appears in one aspect as simple and in another as infinitely complex, the two aspects have by no means the same importance, or rather the same degree of reality. In such cases, the simplicity belongs to the object itself, and the infinite complexity to the views we take in turning around it, to the symbols by which our senses or intellect represent it to us, or, more generally, to elements *of a different order,* with which we try to imitate it artificially, but with which it remains incommensurable, being of a different nature. An artist of genius has painted a figure on his canvas. We can imitate his picture with many-colored squares of mosaic. And we shall reproduce the curves and shades of the model so much the better as our squares are smaller, more numerous and more varied in tone. But an infinity of elements infinitely small, presenting an infinity of shades, would be necessary to obtain the exact equivalent of the figure that the artist has conceived as a simple thing, which he has wished to transport as a whole to the canvas, and which is the more complete the more it strikes us as the projection of an indivisible intuition. Now, suppose our eyes so made that they cannot help seeing in the work of the master a mosaic effect. Or suppose our intellect so made that it cannot explain the appearance of the figure on the canvas except as a work of mosaic. We should then be able to speak simply of a collection of little squares, and we should be under the mechanistic hypothesis. We might add that, besides the materiality of the collection, there must be a plan on which the artist worked; and then we should be expressing ourselves as finalists. But in neither case should we have got at the real process, for there are no squares brought together. It is the picture, *i.e.,* the simple act, projected on the canvas, which, by the mere fact of entering into our perception, is *de*composed before our eyes into thousands and thousands of little squares which present, as *re*composed, a wonderful arrangement. So the eye, with its marvelous complexity of structure, may be only the simple act of vision, divided *for us* into a mosaic of cells, whose order seems marvelous to us because we have conceived the whole as an assemblage. . . .

THE EVOLUTION OF LIFE

The evolution movement would be a simple one, and we should soon have been able to determine its direction, if life had described a single course, like that of a solid ball shot from a cannon. But it proceeds rather like a shell, which suddenly bursts into fragments, which fragments, being themselves shells, burst in their turn into fragments destined to burst again, and so on for a time incommensurably long. We perceive only what is nearest to us, namely, the scattered movements of the pulverized explosions. From them we have to go back, stage by stage, to the original movement.

When a shell bursts, the particular way it breaks is explained both by the explosive force of the powder it contains and by the resistance of the metal. So of the way life breaks into individuals and species. It depends, we think, on two series of causes: the resistance life meets from inert matter, and the explosive force—due to an unstable balance of tendencies—which life bears within itself.

The resistance of inert matter was the obstacle that had first to be overcome. Life seems to have succeeded in this by dint of humility, by making itself very small and very insinuating, bending to physical and chemical forces, consenting even to go a part of the way with them, like the switch that adopts for a while the direction of the rail it is endeavoring to leave. Of phenomena in the simplest forms of life, it is hard to say whether they are still physical and chemical or whether they are already vital. Life had to enter thus into the habits of inert matter, in order to draw it little by little, magnetized, as it were, to another track. The animate forms that first appeared were therefore of extreme simplicity. They were probably tiny masses of scarcely differentiated protoplasm, outwardly resembling the amoeba observable today, but possessed of the tremendous internal push that was to raise them even to the highest forms of life. That in virtue of this push the first organisms sought to grow as much as possible seems likely. But organized matter has a limit of expansion that is very quickly reached; beyond a certain point it divides instead of growing. Ages of effort and prodigies of subtlety were probably necessary for life to get past this new obstacle. It succeeded in inducing an increasing number of elements, ready to divide, to remain united. By the division of labor it knotted between them an indissoluble bond. The complex and quasi-discontinuous organism is thus made to function as would a continuous living mass which had simply grown bigger.

But the real and profound causes of division were those which life bore within its bosom. For life is tendency, and the essence of a tendency is to develop in the form of a sheaf, creating, by its very growth, divergent directions among which its impetus is divided. This we observe in ourselves, in the evolution of that special tendency which we call our character. Each of us, glancing back over his history, will find that his child-personality, though indivisible, united in itself divers persons, which could remain blended just because they were in their nascent state: this indecision, so charged with promise, is one of the greatest charms of childhood. But these interwoven personalities become incompatible in course of growth, and, as each of us can live but one life, a choice must perforce be made. We choose in reality without ceasing; without ceasing, also, we abandon many things. The route we pursue in time is strewn with the remains of all that we began to be, of all that we might have become. But nature, which has at command an incalculable number of lives, is in no wise bound to make such sacrifices. She preserves the different tendencies that have bifurcated with their growth. She creates with them diverging series of species that will evolve separately.

These series may, moreover, be of unequal importance. The author who begins a novel puts into his hero many things which he is obliged to discard as he goes on. Perhaps he will take them up later in other books, and make new characters with them, who will seem like extracts from, or rather like complements of, the first; but they will almost always appear somewhat poor and limited in comparison with the original character. So with regard to the evolution of life. The bifurcations on the way have been numerous, but there have been many blind alleys beside the two or three highways; and of these highways themselves, only one, that which leads through the vertebrates up to man, has been wide enough to allow free passage to the full breath of life. We get this impression when we compare the societies of bees and ants, for instance, with human societies. The former are admirably ordered and united, but stereotyped; the latter are open to every sort of progress, but divided, and incessantly at strife with themselves. The ideal would be a society always in progress and always in equilibrium, but this ideal is perhaps unrealizable: the two characteristics that would fain complete each other, which do complete each other in their embryonic state, can no longer abide together when they grow stronger. If one could speak, otherwise than metaphorically, of an impulse toward social life, it might be said that the brunt of the impulse was borne along the line of evolution ending at man, and that the rest of it was collected on the road leading to the Hymenoptera: the societies of ants and bees would thus present the aspect complementary to ours. But this would be only a manner of expression. There has been no particular impulse toward social life; there is simply the general movement of life, which on divergent lines is creating forms ever new. If societies should appear on two of these lines, they ought to show divergence of paths at the same time as community of impetus. They will thus develop two classes of characteristics which we shall find vaguely complementary of each other.

So our study of the evolution movement will have to unravel a certain number of divergent directions, and to appreciate the importance of what has happened along each of them—in a word, to determine the nature of the dissociated tendencies and estimate their relative proportion. Combining these tendencies, then, we shall get an approximation, or rather an imitation, of the indivisible motor principle whence their impetus proceeds. Evolution will thus prove to be something entirely different from a series of adaptations to circumstances, as mechanism claims; entirely different also from the realization of a plan of the whole, as maintained by the doctrine of finality.

That adaptation to environment is the necessary condition of evolution we do not question for a moment. It is quite evident that a species would disappear, should it fail to bend to the conditions of existence which are imposed on it. But it is one thing to recognize that outer circumstances are forces evolution must reckon with, another to claim that they are the directing causes of evolution. This latter theory is that of mechanism. It excludes absolutely the hypothesis of an original impetus, I mean an internal push that has carried life, by more and more complex forms, to higher and higher destinies. Yet this impetus is evident, and a mere glance at fossil species shows us that life need not have evolved at all, or might have evolved only in very restricted limits, if it had chosen the alternative, much more convenient to itself, of becoming anchylosed in its primitive forms. Certain Foraminifera have not varied since the Silurian epoch. Unmoved witnesses of the innumerable revolutions that have upheaved our planet, the Lingulae are today what they were at the remotest times of the Paleozoic era.

The truth is that adaptation explains the sinuosities of the movement of evolution, but not its general directions, still less the movement itself.[1] The road that leads to the town is obliged to follow the ups and downs of the hills; it *adapts itself* to the accidents of the ground; but the accidents of the ground are not the cause of the road, nor have they given it its direction. At every moment they furnish it with what is indispensable, namely, the soil on which it lies; but if we consider the whole of the road, instead of each of its parts, the accidents of the ground appear only as impediments or causes of delay, for the road aims simply at the town and would fain be a straight line. Just so as regards the evolution of life and the circumstances through which it passes—with this difference, that evolution does not mark out a solitary route, that it takes directions without aiming at ends, and that it remains inventive even in its adaptations.

But, if the evolution of life is something other than a series of adaptations to accidental circumstances, so also it is not the realization of a plan. A plan is given in advance. It is represented, or at least representable, before its realization. The complete execution of it may be put off to a distant future, or even indefinitely; but the idea is none the less formulable at the present time, in terms actually given. If,

[1] This view of adaptation has been noted by M. F. Marin in a remarkable article on the origin of species, "L'Origine des espèces" (*Revue scientifique*, Nov. 1901), p. 580.

on the contrary, evolution is a creation unceasingly renewed, it creates, as it goes on, not only the forms of life, but the ideas that will enable the intellect to understand it, the terms which will serve to express it. That is to say that its future overflows its present, and cannot be sketched out therein in an idea.

There is the first error of finalism. It involves another, yet more serious.

If life realizes a plan, it ought to manifest a greater harmony the further it advances, just as the house shows better and better the idea of the architect as stone is set upon stone. If, on the contrary, the unity of life is to be found solely in the impetus that pushes it along the road of time, the harmony is not in front, but behind. The unity is derived from a *vis a tergo:* it is given at the start as an impulsion, not placed at the end as an attraction. In communicating itself, the impetus splits up more and more. Life, in proportion to its progress, is scattered in manifestations which undoubtedly owe to their common origin the fact that they are complementary to each other in certain aspects, but which are none the less mutually incompatible and antagonistic. So the discord between species will go on increasing. Indeed, we have as yet only indicated the essential cause of it. We have supposed, for the sake of simplicity, that each species received the impulsion in order to pass it on to others, and that, in every direction in which life evolves, the propagation is in a straight line. But, as a matter of fact, there are species which are arrested; there are some that retrogress. Evolution is not only a movement forward; in many cases we observe a marking-time, and still more often a deviation or turning back. It must be so, as we shall show further on, and the same causes that divide the evolution movement often cause life to be diverted from itself, hypnotized by the form it has just brought forth. Thence results an increasing disorder.

No doubt there is progress, if progress mean a continual advance in the general direction determined by a first impulsion, but this progress is accomplished only on the two or three great lines of evolution on which forms ever more and more complex, ever more and more high, appear; between these lines run a crowd of minor paths in which, on the contrary, deviations, arrests, and set-backs, are multiplied. The philosopher, who begins by laying down as a principle that each detail is connected with some general plan of the whole, goes from one disappointment to another as soon as he comes to examine the facts; and, as he had put everything in the same rank, he finds that, as the result of not allowing for accident, he must regard everything as accidental. For accident, then, an allowance must first be made, and a very liberal allowance. We must recognize that all is not coherent in nature. By so doing, we shall be led to ascertain the centers around which the incoherence crystallizes. This crystallization itself will clarify the rest; the main directions will appear, in which life is moving whilst developing the original impulse. True, we shall not witness the detailed accomplishment of a plan. Nature is more and better than a plan in course of realization. A plan is a term assigned to a labor: it closes the future whose form it indicates. Before the evolution of life, on the contrary, the portals of the future remain wide open. It is a creation that goes on forever in virtue of an initial movement. This movement constitutes the unity of the organized world—a prolific unity, of an infinite richness, superior to any that the intellect could dream of, for the intellect is only one of its aspects or products. . . .

INTELLIGENCE AND INSTINCT

So, by different ways, we are led to the same conclusion. The evolution of the arthropods reaches its culminating point

in the insect, and in particular, in the Hymenoptera, as that of
the vertebrates in man. Now, since instinct is nowhere so
developed as in the insect world, and in no group of insects
so marvelously as in the Hymenoptera, it may be said that
the whole evolution of the animal kingdom, apart from retro-
gressions toward vegetative life, has taken place on two
divergent paths, one of which led to instinct and the other to
intelligence.

Vegetative torpor, instinct and intelligence—these, then,
are the elements that coincided in the vital impulsion common to plants and animals, and which, in the course of a
development in which they were made manifest in the most
unforeseen forms, have been dissociated by the very fact of
their growth. *The cardinal error which, from Aristotle on-
wards, has vitiated most of the philosophies of nature, is to
see in vegetative, instinctive and rational life, three successive
degrees of the development of one and the same tendency,
whereas they are three divergent directions of an activity that
has split up as it grew.* The difference between them is not a
difference of intensity, nor, more generally, of degree, but of
kind.

It is important to investigate this point. We have seen in
the case of vegetable and animal life how they are at once
mutually complementary and mutually antagonistic. Now
we must show that intelligence and instinct also are opposite
and complementary. But let us first explain why we are
generally led to regard them as activities of which one is
superior to the other and based upon it, whereas in reality
they are not things of the same order: they have not succeeded one another, nor can we assign to them different
grades.

It is because intelligence and instinct, having originally

been interpenetrating, retain something of their common origin. Neither is ever found in a pure state. We said that in the plant the consciousness and mobility of the animal, which lie dormant, can be awakened; and that the animal lives under the constant menace of being drawn aside to the vegetative life. The two tendencies—that of the plant and that of the animal—were so thoroughly interpenetrating, to begin with, that there has never been a complete severance between them: they haunt each other continually; everywhere we find them mingled; it is the proportion that differs. So with intelligence and instinct. There is no intelligence in which some traces of instinct are not to be discovered, more especially no instinct that is not surrounded with a fringe of intelligence. It is this fringe of intelligence that has been the cause of so many misunderstandings. From the fact that instinct is always more or less intelligent, it has been concluded that instinct and intelligence are things of the same kind, that there is only a difference of complexity of perfection between them, and, above all, that one of the two is expressible in terms of the other. In reality, they accompany each other only because they are complementary, and they are complementary only because they are different, what is instinctive in instinct being opposite to what is intelligent in intelligence.

We are bound to dwell on this point. It is one of the utmost importance.

Let us say at the outset that the distinctions we are going to make will be too sharply drawn, just because we wish to define in instinct what is instinctive, and in intelligence what is intelligent, whereas all concrete instinct is mingled with intelligence, as all real intelligence is penetrated by instinct. Moreover, neither intelligence nor instinct lends itself to rigid definition: they are tendencies, and not things. Also, it must

not be forgotten that in the present chapter we are considering intelligence and instinct as going out of life which de-
posits them along its course. Now the life manifested by an
organism is, in our view, a certain effort to obtain certain
things from the material world. No wonder, therefore, if it
is the diversity of this effort that strikes us in instinct and
intelligence, and if we see in these two modes of psychical
activity, above all else, two different methods of action on
inert matter. This rather narrow view of them has the advantage of giving us an objective means of distinguishing
them. In return, however, it gives us, of intelligence in general and of instinct in general, only the mean position above
and below which both constantly oscillate. For that reason the
reader must expect to see in what follows only a diagram-
matic drawing, in which the respective outlines of intelligence and instinct are sharper than they should be, and in
which the shading-off which comes from the indecision of
each and from their reciprocal encroachment on one another is neglected. In a matter so obscure, we cannot strive too
hard for clearness. It will always be easy afterwards to soften
the outlines and to correct what is too geometrical in the
drawing—in short, to replace the rigidity of a diagram by
the suppleness of life.

To what date is it agreed to ascribe the appearance of
man on the earth? To the period when the first weapons, the
first tools, were made. The memorable quarrel over the discovery of Boucher de Perthes in the quarry of Moulin-
Quignon is not forgotten. The question was whether real
hatchets had been found or merely bits of flint accidentally
broken. But that, supposing they were hatchets, we were indeed in the presence of intelligence, and more particularly
of *human* intelligence, no one doubted for an instant. Now let

us open a collection of anecdotes on the intelligence of animals: we shall see that besides many acts explicable by imitation or by the automatic association of images, there are some that we do not hesitate to call intelligent: foremost among them are those that bear witness to some idea of manufacture, whether the animal life succeeds in fashioning a crude instrument or uses for its profit an object made by man. The animals that rank immediately after man in the matter of intelligence, the apes and elephants, are those that can use an artificial instrument occasionally. Below, but not very far from them, come those that *recognize* a constructed object: for example, the fox, which knows quite well that a trap is a trap. No doubt, there is intelligence wherever there is inference; but inference, which consists in an inflection of past experience in the direction of present experience, is already a beginning of invention. Invention becomes complete when it is materialized in a manufactured instrument. Toward that achievement the intelligence of animals tends as toward an ideal. And though, ordinarily, it does not yet succeed in fashioning artificial objects and in making use of them, it is preparing for this by the very variations which it performs on the instincts furnished by nature. As regards human intelligence, it has not been sufficiently noted that mechanical invention has been from the first its essential feature, that even today our social life gravitates around the manufacture and use of artificial instruments, that the inventions which strew the road of progress have also traced its direction. This we hardly realize, because it takes us longer to change ourselves than to change our tools. Our individual and even social habits survive a good while the circumstances for which they were made, so that the ultimate effects of an invention are not observed until its novelty is already out of sight. A century has elapsed since

the invention of the steam engine, and we are only just beginning to feel the depths of the shock it gave us. But the revolution it has effected in industry has nevertheless upset human
relations altogether. New ideas are arising, new feelings are
on the way to flower. In thousands of years, when, seen from
the distance, only the broad lines of the present age will still
be visible, our wars and our revolutions will count for little,
even supposing they are remembered at all; but the steam
engine, and the procession of inventions of every kind that
accompanied it, will perhaps be spoken of as we speak of the
bronze or of the chipped stone of prehistoric times: it will
serve to define an age.[1] If we could rid ourselves of all pride,
if, to define our species, we kept strictly to what the historic
and the prehistoric periods show us to be the constant characteristic of man and of intelligence, we should say not *Homo
sapiens,* but *Homo faber.* In short, *intelligence, considered
in what seems to be its original feature, is the faculty of manufacturing artificial objects, especially tools to make tools, and
of indefinitely varying the manufacture.*

Now, does an unintelligent animal also possess tools or
machines? Yes, certainly, but here the instrument forms a
part of the body that uses it; and, corresponding to this instrument, there is an *instinct* that knows how to use it. True,
it cannot be maintained that *all* instincts consist in a natural
ability to use an inborn mechanism. Such a definition would
not apply to the instincts which Romanes called "secondary";
and more than one "primary" instinct would not come under
it. But this definition, like that which we have provisionally
given of intelligence, determines at least the ideal limit to-

---

[1] M. Paul Lacombe has laid great stress on the important influence that
great inventions have exercised on the evolution of humanity. (P. Lacombe,
De l'histoire considérée comme science, Paris, 1894. See, in particular,
pp. 168–247.)

ward which the very numerous forms of instinct are travel-
ing. Indeed, it has often been pointed out that most instincts
are only the continuance, or rather the consummation, of the
work of organization itself. Where does the activity of instinct begin? And where does that of nature end? We cannot tell. In the metamorphoses of the larva into the nymph
and into the perfect insect, metamorphoses that often require
appropriate action and a kind of initiative on the part of the
larva, there is no sharp line of demarcation between the instinct of the animal and the organizing work of living matter.
We may say, as we will, either that instinct organizes the instruments it is about to use, or that the process of organization is continued in the instinct that has to use the organ. The
most marvelous instincts of the insect do nothing but develop
its special structure into movements: indeed, where social life
divides the labor among different individuals, and thus al-
lots them different instincts, a corresponding difference of
structure is observed: the polymorphism of ants, bees, wasps
and certain pseudo-neuroptera is well known. Thus, if we
consider only those typical cases in which the complete triumph of intelligence and of instinct is seen, we find this essential difference between them: *instinct perfected is a faculty
of using and even of constructing organized instruments;
intelligence perfected is the faculty of making and using unorganized instruments.*

The advantages and drawbacks of these two modes of
activity are obvious. Instinct finds the appropriate instrument
at hand: this instrument, which makes and repairs itself,
which presents, like all the works of nature, an infinite complexity of detail combined with a marvelous simplicity of
function, does at once, when required, what it is called upon
to do, without difficulty and with a perfection that is often
wonderful. In return, it retains an almost invariable structure,

since a modification of it involves a modification of the species. Instinct is therefore necessarily specialized, being nothing but the utilization of a specific instrument for a specific object. The instrument constructed intelligently, on the contrary, is an imperfect instrument. It costs an effort. It is generally troublesome to handle. But, as it is made of unorganized matter, it can take any form whatsoever, serve any purpose, free the living being from every new difficulty that arises and bestow on it an unlimited number of powers. Whilst it is inferior to the natural instrument for the satisfaction of immediate wants, its advantage over it is the greater, the less urgent the need. Above all, it reacts on the nature of the being that constructs it; for in calling on him to exercise a new function, it confers on him, so to speak, a richer organization, being an artificial organ by which the natural organism is extended. For every need that it satisfies, it creates a new need; and so, instead of closing, like instinct, the round of action within which the animal tends to move automatically, it lays open to activity an unlimited field into which it is driven further and further, and made more and more free. But this advantage of intelligence over instinct only appears at a late stage, when intelligence, having raised construction to a higher degree, proceeds to construct constructive machinery. At the outset, the advantages and drawbacks of the artificial instrument and of the natural instrument balance so well that it is hard to foretell which of the two will secure to the living being the greater empire over nature.

We may surmise that they began by being implied in each other, that the original psychical activity included both at once, and that, if we went far enough back into the past, we should find instincts more nearly approaching intelligence than those of our insects, intelligence nearer to instinct than that of our vertebrates, intelligence and instinct being, in this elementary condition, prisoners of a matter which they are not yet able to control. If the force immanent in life were an unlimited force, it might perhaps have developed instinct and intelligence together, and to any extent, in the same organisms. But everything seems to indicate that this force is limited, and that it soon exhausts itself in its very manifestation. It is hard for it to go far in several directions at once: it must choose. Now, it has the choice between two modes of action on the material world: it can either effect this action *directly* by creating an *organized* instrument to work with; or else it can effect it *indirectly* through an organism which, instead of possessing the required instrument naturally, will itself construct it by fashioning inorganic matter. Hence intelligence and instinct, which diverge more and more as they develop, but which never entirely separate from each other. On the one hand, the most perfect instinct of the insect is accompanied by gleams of intelligence, if only in the choice of place, time and materials of construction: the bees, for example, when by exception they build in the open air, invent new and really intelligent arrangements to adapt themselves to such new conditions.[1] But, on the other hand, intelligence has even more need of instinct than instinct has of intelligence; for the power to give shape to crude matter involves already a superior degree of organization, a degree to which the animal could not have risen, save on the wings of instinct. So, while nature has frankly evolved in the direction of instinct in the arthropods, we observe in almost all the vertebrates the striving after rather than the expansion of intelligence. It is instinct still which forms the basis of their psychical activity; but intelligence is there, and would fain supersede it. Intelligence does not yet succeed in inventing instru-

[1] Bouvier, "La Nidification des abeilles à l'air libre" (*C.R. de l'Ac. des sciences,* 7 mai 1906).

ments; but at least it tries to, by performing as many variations as possible on the instinct which it would like to dispense with. It gains complete self-possession only in man, and this triumph is attested by the very insufficiency of the natural means at man's disposal for defense against his enemies, against cold and hunger. This insufficiency, when we strive to fathom its significance, acquired the value of a prehistoric document; it is the final leave-taking between intelligence and instinct. But it is no less true that nature must have hesitated between two modes of psychical activity—one assured of immediate success, but limited in its effects; the other hazardous, but whose conquests, if it should reach independence, might be extended indefinitely. Here again, then, the greatest success was achieved on the side of the greatest risk. *Instinct and intelligence therefore represent two divergent solutions, equally fitting, of one and the same problem. . . .*

. . . The intellect is not made to think *evolution,* in the proper sense of the word—that is to say, the continuity of a change that is pure mobility. We shall not dwell here on this point, which we propose to study in a special chapter. Suffice it to say that the intellect represents *becoming* as a series of *states,* each of which is homogeneous with itself and consequently does not change. Is our attention called to the internal change of one of these states? At once we decompose it into another series of states which, reunited, will be supposed to make up this internal modification. Each of these new states must be invariable, or else their internal change, if we are forced to notice it, must be resolved again into a fresh series of invariable states, and so on to infinity. Here again, thinking consists in reconstituting, and, naturally, it is with *given* elements, and consequently with *stable* elements, that we reconstitute. So that, though we may do our best to imitate the mobility of becoming by an addition that is ever going on, becoming itself slips through our fingers just when we think we are holding it tight.

Precisely because it is always trying to reconstitute, and to reconstitute with what is given, the intellect lets what is *new* in each moment of a history escape. It does not admit the unforeseeable. It rejects all creation. That definite antecedents bring forth a definite consequent, calculable as a function of them, is what satisfies our intellect. That a definite end calls forth definite means to attain it, is what we also understand. In both cases we have to do with the known which is combined with the known, in short, with the old which is repeated. Our intellect is there at its ease; and, whatever be the object, it will abstract, separate, eliminate, so as to substitute for the object itself, if necessary, an approximate equivalent in which things will happen in this way. But that each instant is a fresh endowment, that the new is ever upspringing, that the form just come into existence (although, *when once produced,* it may be regarded as an effect determined by its causes) could never have been foreseen—because the causes here, unique in their kind, are part of the effect, have come into existence with it, and are determined by it as much as they determine it—all this we can feel within ourselves and also divine, by sympathy, outside ourselves, but we cannot think it, in the strict sense of the word, nor express it in terms of pure understanding. No wonder at that: we must remember what our intellect is meant for. The causality it seeks and finds everywhere expresses the very mechanism of our industry, in which we go on recomposing the same whole with the same parts, repeating the same movements to obtain the same result. The finality it understands best is the finality of our industry, in which we work on a model given in advance, that is to say, old or composed of elements already known. As to invention properly so called, which is, however, the point of departure of industry itself, our intellect does not succeed in grasping it in its *upspringing,* that is to say, in its indivisibility, nor in its *fervor,* that is to say, in its creativeness. Explaining it always consists in resolving it, it the unforeseeable and new, into elements old or known, arranged in a different order. The intellect can no more admit complete novelty than real becoming; that is to say, here again it lets an essential aspect of life escape, as if it were not intended to think such an object.

All our analyses bring us to this conclusion. But it is hardly necessary to go into such long details concerning the mechanism of intellectual working; it is enough to consider the results. We see that the intellect, so skilful in dealing with the inert, is awkward the moment it touches the living. Whether it wants to treat the life of the body or the life of the mind, it proceeds with the rigor, the stiffness and the brutality of an instrument not designed for such use. The history of hygiene or of pedagogy teaches us much in this matter. When we think of the cardinal, urgent and constant need we have to preserve our bodies and to raise our souls, of the special facilities given to each of us, in this field, to experiment continually on ourselves and on others, of the palpable injury by which the wrongness of a medical or pedagogical practice is both made manifest and punished at once, we are amazed at the stupidity and especially at the persistence of errors. We may easily find their origin in the natural obstinacy with which we treat the living like the lifeless and think all reality, however fluid, under the form of the sharply defined solid. We are at ease only in the discontinuous, in the immobile, in the dead. *The intellect is characterized by a natural inability to comprehend life. . . .*

ORDER AND DISORDER

Our standards of measurement are conventional, and, so to say, foreign to the intentions of nature: can we suppose that nature has related all the modalities of heat to the expansion of the same mass of mercury, or to the change of pressure of the same mass of air kept at a constant volume? But we may go further. In a general way, *measuring* is a wholly human operation, which implies that we really or ideally superpose two objects one on another a certain number of times. Nature did not dream of this superposition. It does not measure, nor does it count. Yet physics counts, measures, relates "quantitative" variations to one another to obtain laws, and it succeeds. Its success would be inexplicable, if the movement which constitutes materiality were not the same movement which, prolonged by us to its end, that is to say, to homogeneous space, results in making us count, measure, follow in their respective variations terms that are functions one of another. To effect this prolongation of the movement, our intellect has only to let itself go, for it runs naturally to space and mathematics, intellectuality and materiality being of the same nature and having been produced in the same way.

If the mathematical order were a positive thing, if there were, immanent in matter, laws comparable to those of our codes, the success of our science would have in it something of the miraculous. What chances should we have indeed of finding the standard of nature and of isolating exactly, in order to determine their reciprocal relations, the very variables which nature has chosen? But the success of a science of mathematical form would be no less incomprehensible, if matter did not already possess everything necessary to adapt itself to our formulae. One hypothesis only, therefore, remains plausible, namely, that the mathematical order is nothing positive, that it is the form toward which a certain *interruption* tends of itself, and that materiality consists precisely in an interruption of this kind. We shall understand then why our science is contingent, relative to the variables it has chosen, relative to the order in which it has successively put the problems, and why nevertheless it succeeds. It might have been, as a whole, altogether different, and yet have succeeded. This is so, just because there is no definite system of mathematical laws, at the base of nature, and because mathematics in general represents simply the side to which matter inclines. Put one of those little cork dolls with leaden feet in any posture, lay it on its back, turn it up on its head, throw it into the air: it will always stand itself up again, automatically. So likewise with matter: we can take it by any end and handle it in any way, it will always fall back into some one of our mathematical formulae, because it is weighted with geometry.

But the philosopher will perhaps refuse to found a theory of knowledge on such considerations. They will be repugnant to him, because the mathematical order, being order, will appear to him to contain something positive. It is in vain that we assert that this order produces itself automatically by the interruption of the inverse order, that it is this very interruption. The idea persists, none the less, that *there might be no order at all,* and that the mathematical order of things, being a conquest over disorder, possesses a positive reality. In examining this point, we shall see what a prominent part the idea of *disorder* plays in problems relative to the theory of knowledge. It does not appear explicitly, and that is why it escapes our attention. It is, however, with the criticism of this idea that a theory of knowledge ought to begin, for if the great problem is to know why and how reality submits itself to an order, it is because the absence of every kind of order appears possible or conceivable. It is this absence of order that realists and idealists alike believe they are thinking of—the realist when he speaks of the regularity that "objective" laws actually impose on a virtual disorder of nature, the idealist when he supposes a "sensuous manifold" which is coördinated (and consequently itself without order) under the organizing influence of our understanding. The idea of disorder, in the sense of *absence of order,* is then what must be analyzed first. Philosophy borrows it from daily life. And it is unquestionable that, when ordinarily we speak of disorder, we are thinking of something. But of what?

It will be seen in the next chapter how hard it is to determine the content of a negative idea, and what illusions one is liable to, what hopeless difficulties philosophy falls into, for not having undertaken this task. Difficulties and illusions are generally due to this, that we accept as final a manner of expression essentially provisional. They are due to our bringing into the domain of speculation a procedure made for practice. If I choose a volume in my library at random, I may put it back on the shelf after glancing at it and say, "This is not verse." Is this what I have really seen in turning over the leaves of the book? Obviously not. I have not seen, I never shall see, an absence of verse. I have seen prose. But as it is poetry I want, I express what I find as a function of what I am looking for, and instead of saying, "This is prose," I say, "This is not verse." In the same way, if the fancy takes me to read prose, and I happen on a volume of verse, I shall say, "This is not prose," thus expressing the data of my perception, which shows me verse, in the language of my expectation and attention, which are fixed on the idea of prose and will hear of nothing else. Now, if M. Jourdain heard me, he would infer, no doubt, from my two exclamations that prose and poetry are two forms of language reserved for books, and that these learned forms have come and overlaid a language which was neither prose nor verse. Speaking of this thing which is neither verse nor prose, he would suppose, moreover, that he was thinking of it: it would be only a pseudo-idea, however. Let us go further still: the pseudo-idea would create a pseudo-problem, if M. Jourdain were to ask his professor of philosophy how the prose form and the poetry form have been superadded to that which possessed neither the one nor the other, and if he wished the professor to construct a theory of the imposition of these two forms upon this formless matter. His question would be absurd, and the absurdity would lie in this, that he was hypostatizing as the substratum of prose and poetry the simultaneous negation of both, forgetting that the negation of the one consists in the affirmation of the other.

Now, suppose that there are two species of order, and that these two orders are two contraries within one and the same genus. Suppose also that the idea of disorder arises in our mind whenever, seeking one of the two kinds of order, we find the other. The idea of disorder would then have a clear meaning in the current practice of life: it would objectify, for the convenience of language, the disappointment of a mind that finds before it an order different from what it wants, an order with which it is not concerned at the moment, and which, in this sense, does not exist for it. But the idea would not admit a theoretical use. So if we claim, notwithstanding, to introduce it into philosophy, we shall inevitably lose sight of its true meaning. It denotes the absence of a certain order, but *to the profit of another* (with which we are not concerned); only, as it applies to each of the two in turn, and as it even goes and comes continually between the two, we take it on the way, or rather on the wing, like a shuttlecock between two battledores, and treat it as if it represented, not the absence of the one or other order as the case may be, but the absence of both together—a thing that is neither perceived nor conceived, a simple verbal entity. So there arises the problem how order is imposed on disorder, form on matter. In analyzing the idea of disorder thus subtilized, we shall see that it represents nothing at all, and at the same time the problems that have been raised around it will vanish.

It is true that we must begin by distinguishing, and even by opposing one to the other, two kinds of order which we generally confuse. As this confusion has created the principal difficulties of the problem of knowledge, it will not be useless to dwell once more on the marks by which the two orders are distinguished.

In a general way, reality is *ordered* exactly to the degree in which it satisfies our thought. Order is therefore a certain agreement between subject and object. It is the mind finding itself again in things. But the mind, we said, can go in two opposite ways. Sometimes it follows its natural direction: there is then progress in the form of tension, continuous creation, free activity. Sometimes it inverts it, and this inversion, pushed to the end, leads to extension, to the necessary reciprocal determination of elements externalized each by relation to the others, in short, to geometrical mechanism. Now, whether experience seems to us to adopt the first direction or whether it is drawn in the direction of the second, in both cases we say there is order, for in the two processes the mind finds itself again. The confusion between them is therefore natural. To escape it, different names would have to be given to the kinds of order, and that is not easy, because of the variety and variability of the forms they take. The order of the second kind may be defined as geometry, which is its extreme limit; more generally, it is that kind of order that is concerned whenever a relation of necessary determination is found between causes and effects. It evokes ideas of inertia, of passivity, of automatism. As to the first kind of order, it oscillates no doubt around finality; and yet we cannot define it as finality, for it is sometimes above, sometimes below. In its highest forms, it is more than finality, for of a free action or a work of art we may say that they show a perfect order, and yet they can only be expressed in terms of ideas approximately, and after the event. Life in its entirety, regarded as a creative evolution, is something analogous; it transcends finality, if we understand by finality the realization of an idea conceived or conceivable in advance. The category of finality is therefore too narrow for life in its entirety. It is, on the other hand, often too wide for a particular manifestation of life taken separately. Be that as it may, it is with the *vital* that we have here to do, and the whole present study strives to prove that the vital is in the direction of the voluntary. We may say then that this first kind of order is that of the *vital* or of the *willed,* in opposition to the second, which is that of the *inert* and the *automatic*. Common sense instinctively distinguishes between the two kinds of order, at least in the extreme cases; instinctively, also, it brings them together. We say of astronomical phenomena that they manifest an admirable order, meaning by this that they can be foreseen mathematically. And we find an order no less admirable in a symphony of Beethoven, which is genius, originality, and therefore unforeseeability itself. . . .

IDEAL GENESIS OF MATTER

Let us imagine a vessel full of steam at a high pressure, and here and there in its sides a crack through which the steam is escaping in a jet. The steam thrown into the air is nearly all condensed into little drops which fall back, and this condensation and this fall represent simply the loss of something, an interruption, a deficit. But a small part of the jet of steam subsists, uncondensed, for some seconds; it is making an effort to raise the drops which are falling; it succeeds at most in retarding their fall. So, from an immense reservoir of life, jets must be gushing out unceasingly, of which each, falling back, is a world. The evolution of living species within this world represents what subsists of the primitive direction of the original jet, and of an impulsion which continues itself in a direction the inverse of materiality. But let us not carry too far this comparison. It gives us but a feeble and even deceptive image of reality, for the crack, the jet of steam, the forming of the drops, are determined necessarily, whereas the creation of a world is a free act, and the life within the material world participates in this liberty. Let us think rather of an action like that of raising the arm; then let us suppose that the arm, left to itself, falls back, and yet that there subsists in it, striving to raise it up again, something of the will that animates it. In this image of a *creative action which unmakes itself* we have already a more exact representation of matter. In vital activity we see, then, that which subsists of the direct movement in the inverted movement, *a reality which is making itself in a reality which is unmaking itself.*

Everything is obscure in the idea of creation if we think of *things* which are created and a *thing* which creates, as we habitually do, as the understanding cannot help doing. We shall show the origin of this illusion in our next chapter. It is natural to our intellect, whose function is essentially practical, made to present to us things and states rather than changes and acts. But things and states are only views, taken by our mind, of becoming. There are no things, there are only actions. More particularly, if I consider the world in which we live, I find that the automatic and strictly determined evolution of this well-knit whole is action which is unmaking itself, and that the unforeseen forms which life cuts out in it, forms capable of being themselves prolonged into unforeseen movements, represent the action that is making itself. Now, I have every reason to believe that the other worlds are analogous to ours, that things happen there in the same way. And I know they were not all constructed at the same time, since observation shows me, even today, nebulae in course of concentration. Now, if the same kind of action is going on everywhere, whether it is that which is unmaking itself or whether it is that which is striving to remake itself, I simply express this probable similitude when I speak of a center from which worlds shoot out like rockets in a fireworks display—provided, however, that I do not present this center as a *thing,* but as a continuity of shooting out. God thus defined, has nothing of the already made; He is unceasing life, action, freedom. Creation, so conceived, is not a mystery; we experience it in ourselves when we act freely. That new things can join things already existing is absurd, no doubt, since the *thing* results from a solidification performed by our understanding, and there are never any things other than those that the understanding has thus constituted. To speak of things creating themselves would therefore amount to saying that the understanding presents to itself more than it presents to itself—a self-contradictory affirmation, an empty and vain idea. But that action increases as it goes on, that it creates in the measure of its advance, is what each of us finds when he watches himself act. Things are constituted by the instantaneous cut which the understanding practices, at a given moment, on a flux of this kind, and what is mysterious when we compare the cuts together becomes clear when we relate them to the flux. Indeed, the modalities of creative action, in so far as it is still going on in the organization of living forms, are much simplified

when they are taken in this way. Before the complexity of
an organism and the practically infinite multitude of interwoven analyses and syntheses it presupposes, our understanding recoils disconcerted. That the simple play of physical
and chemical forces, left to themselves, should have worked
this marvel, we find hard to believe. And if it is a profound
science which is at work, how are we to understand the influence exercised on this matter without form by this form
without matter? But the difficulty arises from this, that we
represent statically ready-made material particles juxtaposed
to one another, and, also statically, an external cause which
plasters upon them a skilfully contrived organization. In
reality, life is a movement, materiality is the inverse movement, and each of these two movements is simple, the matter
which forms a world being an undivided flux, and undivided
also the life that runs through it, cutting out in it living beings
all along its track. Of these two currents the second runs
counter to the first, but the first obtains, all the same, something from the second. There results between them a *modus
vivendi,* which is organization. This organization takes, for
our senses and for our intellect, the form of parts entirely external to other parts in space and in time. Not only do we
shut our eyes to the unity of the impulse which, passing
through generations, links individuals with individuals,
species with species, and makes of the whole series of the
living one single immense wave flowing over matter, but
each individual itself seems to us as an aggregate; aggregate
of molecules and aggregate of facts. The reason of this lies
in the structure of our intellect, which is formed to act on
matter from without, and which succeeds by making, in the
flux of the real, instantaneous cuts, each of which becomes,
in its fixity, endlessly decomposable. Perceiving, in an organism, only parts external to parts, the understanding has the

choice between two systems of explanation only: either to regard the infinitely complex (and thereby infinitely well-contrived) organization as a fortuitous concatenation of atoms, or to relate it to the incomprehensible influence of an external force that has grouped its elements together. But this complexity is the work of the understanding; this incomprehensibility is also its work. Let us try to see, no longer with the eyes of the intellect alone, which grasps only the already made and which looks from the outside, but with the spirit, I mean with that faculty of seeing which is immanent in the faculty of acting and which springs up, somehow, by the twisting of the will on itself, when action is turned into knowledge, like heat, so to say, into light. To movement, then, everything will be restored, and into movement everything will be resolved. Where the understanding, working on the image supposed to be fixed of the progressing action, shows us parts infinitely manifold and an order infinitely well contrived, we catch a glimpse of a simple process, an action which is making itself across an action of the same kind which is unmaking itself, like the fiery path torn by the last rocket of a fireworks display through the black cinders of the spent rockets that are falling dead. . . .

THE MEANING OF EVOLUTION

. . . How can we help being struck by the fact that, while man is capable of learning any sort of exercise, of constructing any sort of object, in short of acquiring any kind of motor habit whatsoever, the faculty of combining new movements is strictly limited in the best-endowed animal, even in the ape? The cerebral characteristic of man is there. The human brain is made, like every brain, to set up motor mechanisms and to enable us to choose among them, at any instant, the one we shall put in motion by the pull of a trigger. But it

differs from other brains in this, that the number of mechanisms it can set up, and consequently the choice that it gives
as to which among them shall be released, is unlimited. Now,
from the limited to the unlimited there is all the distance
between the closed and the open. It is not a difference of degree, but of kind.

Radical therefore, also, is the difference between animal
consciousness, even the most intelligent, and human consciousness. For consciousness corresponds exactly to the living
being's power of choice; it is coextensive with the fringe of
possible action that surrounds the real action: consciousness
is synonymous with invention and with freedom. Now, in
the animal, invention is never anything but a variation on
the theme of routine. Shut up in the habits of the species,
it succeeds, no doubt, in enlarging them by its individual
initiative; but it escapes automatism only for an instant, for
just the time to create a new automatism. The gates of its
prison close as soon as they are opened; by pulling at its chain
it succeeds only in stretching it. With man, consciousness
breaks the chain. In man, and in man alone, it sets itself free.
The whole history of life until man has been that of the
effort of consciousness to raise matter, and of the more or
less complete overwhelming of consciousness by the matter
which has fallen back on it. The enterprise was paradoxical,
if, indeed, we may speak here otherwise than by metaphor
of enterprise and of effort. It was to create with matter, which
is necessity itself, an instrument of freedom, to make a machine which should triumph over mechanism, and to use
the determinism of nature to pass through the meshes of the
net which this very determinism had spread. But, everywhere except in man, consciousness has let itself be caught
in the net whose meshes it tried to pass through: it has remained the captive of the mechanisms it has set up. Autom-

atism, which it tries to draw in the direction of freedom, winds about it and drags it down. It has not the power to escape, because the energy it has provided for acts is almost all employed in maintaining the infinitely subtle and essentially unstable equilibrium into which it has brought matter. But man not only maintains his machine, he succeeds in using it as he pleases. Doubtless he owes this to the superiority of his brain, which enables him to build an unlimited number of motor mechanisms, to oppose new habits to the old ones unceasingly, and, by dividing automatism against itself, to rule it. He owes it to his language, which furnishes consciousness with an immaterial body in which to incarnate itself and thus exempts it from dwelling exclusively on material bodies, whose flux would soon drag it along and finally swallow it up. He owes it to social life, which stores and preserves efforts as language stores thought, fixes thereby a mean level to which individuals must raise themselves at the outset, and by this initial stimulation prevents the average man from slumbering and drives the superior man to mount still higher. But our brain, our society, and our language are only the external and various signs of one and the same internal superiority. They tell, each after its manner, the unique, exceptional success which life has won at a given moment of its evolution. They express the difference of kind, and not only of degree, which separates man from the rest of the animal world. They let us guess that, while at the end of the vast spring-board from which life has taken its leap, all the others have stepped down, finding the cord stretched too high, man alone has cleared the obstacle.

It is in this quite special sense that man is the "term" and the "end" of evolution. Life, we have said, transcends finality as it transcends the other categories. It is essentially a current sent through matter, drawing from it what it can. There has not, therefore, properly speaking, been any project or plan. On the other hand, it is abundantly evident that the rest of nature is not for the sake of man: we struggle like the other species, we have struggled against other species. Moreover, if the evolution of life had encountered other accidents in its course, if, thereby, the current of life had been otherwise divided, we should have been, physically and morally, far different from what we are. For these various reasons it would be wrong to regard humanity, such as we have it before our eyes, as pre-figured in the evolutionary movement. It cannot even be said to be the outcome of the whole of evolution, for evolution has been accomplished on several divergent lines, and while the human species is at the end of one of them, other lines have been followed with other species at their end. It is in a quite different sense that we hold humanity to be the ground of evolution.

From our point of view, life appears in its entirety as an immense wave which, starting from a center, spreads outwards, and which on almost the whole of its circumference is stopped and converted into oscillation: at one single point the obstacle has been forced, the impulsion has passed freely. It is this freedom that the human form registers. Everywhere but in man, consciousness has had to come to a stand; in man alone it has kept on its way. Man, then, continues the vital movement indefinitely, although he does not draw along with him all that life carries in itself. On other lines of evolution there have traveled other tendencies which life implied, and of which, since everything interpenetrates, man has, doubtless, kept something, but of which he has kept only very little. *It is as if a vague and formless being, whom we may call, as we will,* man or superman, *had sought to realize himself, and had succeeded only by abandoning a part of himself on the way.* The losses are represented by the rest of the animal world, and even by the vegetable world, at least in what these have that is positive and above the accidents of evolution. . . .

. . . A different evolution might have led to a humanity either more intellectual still or more intuitive. In the humanity of which we are a part, intuition is, in fact, almost completely sacrificed to intellect. It seems that to conquer matter, and to reconquer its own self, consciousness has had to exhaust the best part of its power. This conquest, in the particular conditions in which it has been accomplished, has required that consciousness should adapt itself to the habits of matter and concentrate all its attention on them, in fact determine itself more especially as intellect. Intuition is there, however, but vague and above all discontinuous. It is a lamp almost extinguished, which only glimmers now and then, for a few moments at most. But it glimmers wherever a vital interest is at stake. On our personality, on our liberty, on the place we occupy in the whole of nature, on our origin and perhaps also on our destiny, it throws a light feeble and vacillating, but which none the less pierces the darkness of the night in which the intellect leaves us.

These fleeting intuitions, which light up their object only at distant intervals, philosophy ought to seize, first to sustain them, then to expand them and so unite them together. The more it advances in this work, the more will it perceive that intuition is mind itself, and, in a certain sense, life itself: the intellect has been cut out of it by a process resembling that which has generated matter. Thus is revealed the unity of the spiritual life. We recognize it only when we place ourselves in intuition it order to go from intuition to the intellect, for from the intellect we shall never pass to intuition.

Philosophy introduces us thus into the spiritual life. And

it shows us at the same time the relation of the life of the spirit to that of the body. The great error of the doctrines on the spirit has been the idea that by isolating the spiritual life from all the rest, by suspending it in space as high as possible above the earth, they were placing it beyond attack, as if they were not thereby simply exposing it to be taken as an effect of mirage! Certainly they are right to listen to conscience when conscience affirms human freedom; but the intellect is there, which says that the cause determines its effect, that like conditions like, that all is repeated and that all is · given. They are right to believe in the absolute reality of the person and in his independence toward matter; but science is there, which shows the interdependence of conscious life and cerebral activity. They are right to attribute to man a privileged place in nature, to hold that the distance is infinite between the animal and man; but the history of life is there, which makes us witness the genesis of species by gradual transformation, and seems thus to reintegrate man in animality. When a strong instinct assures the probability of personal survival, they are right not to close their ears to its voice; but if there exist "souls" capable of an independent life, whence do they come? When, how and why do they enter into this body which we see arise, quite naturally, from a mixed cell derived from the bodies of its two parents? All these questions will remain unanswered, a philosophy of intuition will be a negation of science, will be sooner or later swept away by science, if it does not resolve to see the life of the body just where it really is, on the road that leads to the life of the spirit. But it will then no longer have to do with definite living beings. Life as a whole, from the initial impulsion that thrust it into the world, will appear as a wave which rises, and which is opposed by the descending movement of matter. On the greater part of its surface, at different

heights, the current is converted by matter into a vortex. At
one point alone it passes freely, dragging with it the obstacle
which will weigh on its progress but will not stop it. At this
point is humanity: it is our privileged situation. On the
other hand, this rising wave is consciousness, and, like all
consciousness, it includes potentialities without number
which interpenetrate and to which consequently neither the
category of unity nor that of multiplicity is appropriate,
made as they both are for inert matter. The matter that it
bears along with it, and in the interstices of which it inserts
itself, alone can divide it into distinct individualities. On
flows the current, running through human generations, subdividing itself into individuals. This subdivision was vaguely
indicated in it, but could not have been made clear without
matter. Thus souls are continually being created, which,
nevertheless, in a certain sense pre-existed. They are nothing
else than the little rills into which the great river of life
divides itself, flowing through the body of humanity. The
movement of the stream is distinct from the river bed, although it must adopt its winding course. Consciousness is
distinct from the organism it animates, although it must
undergo its vicissitudes. As the possible actions which a state
of consciousness indicates are at every instant beginning to
be carried out in the nervous centers, the brain underlies at
every instant the motor indications of the state of consciousness; but the interdependency of consciousness and brain is
limited to this; the destiny of consciousness is not bound up
on that account with the destiny of cerebral matter. Finally,
consciousness is essentially free; it is freedom itself; but it
cannot pass through matter without settling on it, without
adapting itself to it: this adaptation is what we call intellectuality; and the intellect, turning itself back toward active,
that is to say free, consciousness, naturally makes it enter

into the conceptual forms into which it is accustomed to see matter fit. It will therefore always perceive freedom in the form of necessity; it will always neglect the part of novelty or of creation inherent in the free act; it will always substitute for action itself an imitation artificial, approximative, obtained by compounding the old with the old and the same with the same. Thus, to the eyes of a philosophy that attempts to reabsorb intellect in intuition, many difficulties vanish or become light. But such a doctrine does not only facilitate speculation; it gives us also more power to act and to live. For, with it, we feel ourselves no longer isolated in humanity, humanity no longer seems isolated in the nature that it dominates. As the smallest grain of dust is bound up with our entire solar system, drawn along with it in that undivided movement of descent which is materiality itself, so all organized beings, from the humblest to the highest, and from the first origins of life to the time in which we are, and in all places as in all times, do but evidence a single impulsion, the inverse of the movement of matter, and in itself indivisible. All the living hold together, and all yield to the same tremendous push. The animal takes its stand on the plant, man bestrides animality, and the whole of humanity, in space and time, is one immense army galloping beside and before and behind each of us in an overwhelming charge able to beat down every resistance and clear the most formidable obstacles, perhaps even death.

PHILOSOPHICAL INTUITION [1]

Translated by MABELLE L. ANDISON

There is a certain conception of philosophy which requires
that all the effort of the philosopher should be to embrace
in one large synthesis the results of the particular sciences.
Indeed, the philosopher, for a long time, was he who possessed universal knowledge; and today even, when the multiplicity of particular sciences, the diversity and complexity
of methods, the enormous mass of facts collected make the
accumulation of all human knowledge in a single mind impossible, the philosopher remains the man of universal
knowledge, in this sense, that if he can no longer know
everything, there is nothing that he should not have put
himself in a position to learn. But does it necessarily follow,
that his task is to take possession of existing science to bring
it to increasing degrees of generality, and to proceed, from
condensation to condensation, to what has been called the
unification of knowledge? May I be pardoned if I consider
it strange that this conception of philosophy is proposed to
us in the name of science, out of respect for science: I know
of no conception more offensive to science or more injurious
to the scientist. Here, if you like, is a man who, over a long
period of time, has followed a certain scientific method and

[1] Lecture at the Philosophical Congress in Bologna, April 10, 1911. Published in English in Henri Bergson, *The Creative Mind*, trans. by Mabelle L.
Andison (New York, The Philosophical Library, 1946), pp. 144–152.

laboriously gained his results, who says to us: "Experience, with the help of reasoning, leads to this point; scientific knowledge begins here, it ends there; such are my conclusions"; and the philosopher would have the right to answer: "Very well, leave it to me, and I'll show you what I can do with it! The knowledge you bring me unfinished, I shall complete. What you put before me in bits I shall put together. With the same materials, since it is understood that I shall keep to the facts which you have observed, with the same kind of work, since I must restrict myself as you did to induction and deduction, I shall do more and better than you have done." Truly a very strange pretension! How could the profession of philosopher confer upon him who exercises it the power of advancing farther than science in the same direction as science? That certain scientists are more inclined than others to forge ahead and to generalize their results, more inclined also to turn back and criticize their methods, that in this particular meaning of the word they should be dubbed philosophers, moreover that each science can and should have its own philosophy thus understood, I am the first to admit. But that particular philosophy is still science, and he who practices it is still a scientist. It is no longer a question, as it was a moment ago, of setting up philosophy as a synthesis of the positive sciences and of claiming, in virtue of the philosopher's mind alone, to raise oneself above science in the generalization of the same facts.

Such a conception of the rôle of the philosopher would be unfair to science. But how much more unfair to philosophy! Is it not evident that if the scientist stops at a certain point along the road of generalization and synthesis, it is because beyond that point objective experience and sure reasoning do not permit us to advance? And hence in claiming to go further in the same direction, should we not be placing ourselves systematically in the arbitrary or at least the hypothetical? To make of philosophy an ensemble of generalities which goes beyond scientific generalization, is to insist that the philosopher be content with the plausible and that probability be sufficient for him. I am perfectly well aware that for most of those who follow our discussions from a distance, our domain is in fact that of the simple possible, at most that of the probable; they would be very much inclined to say that philosophy begins where certitude leaves off. But who among us would like philosophy to be in such a situation? Doubtless everything is not equally verified or verifiable in what a philosophy brings us, and it is the essence of the philosophical method to demand that at many moments, on many points, the mind should take risks. But the philosopher runs these risks only because he has insured himself and because there are things of which he feels himself unshakably certain. He will make us certain in our turn to the extent that he is able to communicate to us the intuition from whence he draws his strength.

The truth is that philosophy is not a synthesis of particular sciences, and that if it often places itself on the terrain of science, if it sometimes embraces in a simpler vision the objects of science, it is not by intensifying science, it is not by carrying the results of science to a higher degree of generality. There would not be place for two ways of knowing, philosophy and science, if experience did not present itself to us under two different aspects; on the one hand in the form of facts side by side with other facts, which repeat themselves more or less, which can to a certain extent be measured, and which in fact open out in the direction of distinct multiplicity and spatiality; on the other hand in the form of a reciprocal penetration which is pure duration, refractory to law and measurement. In both cases, experience signifies consciousness; but in the first case, consciousness unfolds outward and externalizes itself in relation to itself in the exact measure to which it perceives things as external to one another; in the second, it turns back within itself, it takes possession of itself and develops in depth. In thus probing its own depth does it penetrate more deeply into the interior of matter, of life, or reality in general? One could dispute this if consciousness had been superadded to matter as an accident; but I believe I have shown that such a hypothesis, according to the way in which it is generally taken, is absurd or false, self-contradictory or contradicted by the facts. One might still dispute it, if human consciousness, although related to a higher and vaster consciousness, had been put aside, as if man had to stand in a corner of nature like a child being punished. But no! the matter and life which fill the world are equally within us; the forces which work in all things we feel within ourselves; whatever may be the inner essence of what is and what is done, we are of that essence. Let us then go down into our own inner selves: the deeper the point we touch, the stronger will be the thrust which sends us back to the surface. Philosophical intuition is this contact, philosophy is this impetus. Brought back to the surface by an impulsion from the depth, we shall regain contact with science as our thought opens out and disperses. Philosophy then must be able to model itself upon science, and an idea of so-called intuitive origin which could not manage, by dividing itself and subdividing its divisions, to cover the facts observed outwardly and the laws by which science joins them to each other, which would not be capable even of correcting certain generalizations and of rectifying certain observations, would be pure fantasy; it would have nothing in common with intuition. But on the other hand the idea which succeeds in fitting perfectly this dispersion of itself upon the facts and laws, was not obtained by a unification of external experience; for the philosopher did not arrive at unity, he started from it. I am speaking, naturally, of a unity which is at once restricted and relative, like the unity which marks off a living being from the rest of the universe. The process by which philosophy seems to assimilate the results of positive science, like the operation in the course of which a philosophy appears to re-assemble in itself the fragments of earlier philosophies, is not a synthesis but an analysis.

Science is the auxiliary of action. And action aims at a result. The scientific intelligence asks itself therefore what will have to be done in order that a certain desired result be attained, or more generally, what conditions should obtain in order that a certain phenomenon take place. It goes from an arrangement of things to a re-arrangement, from a simultaneity to a simultaneity. Of necessity it neglects what happens in the interval; or if it does concern itself with it, it is in order to consider other arrangements in it, still more simultaneities. With methods meant to seize the ready-made, it cannot in general enter into what is being done, it cannot follow the moving reality, adopt the becoming which is the life of things. This last task belongs to philosophy. While the scientist, obliged to take immobile views of movement and to gather repetitions along a path where nothing is repeated, intent also upon dividing reality conveniently on successive planes where it is deployed in order to submit it to the action of man, is obliged to use craft with nature, to adopt toward it the wary attitude of an adversary, the philosopher treats nature as a comrade. The rule of science is the one posited by Bacon: obey in order to command. The philosopher neither obeys nor commands; he seeks to be at one with nature. From this point of view, moreover, the essence of philosophy is the spirit of simplicity. Whether we contemplate the philosophi-

cal spirit in itself or in its works, whether we compare philosophy to science or one philosophy with other philosophies,
we always find that any complication is superficial, that the
construction is a mere accessory, synthesis a semblance: the
act of philosophizing is a simple one. . . .

Intuition doubtless admits of many degrees of intensity,
and philosophy many degrees of depth; but the mind once
brought back to real duration will already be alive with intuitive life and its knowledge of things will already be philosophy. Instead of a discontinuity of movements replacing
one another in an infinitely divided time, it will perceive the
continuous fluidity of real time which flows along, indivisible.
Instead of surface states covering successively some neutral
stuff and maintaining with it a mysterious relationship of
phenomenon to substance, it will seize upon one identical
change which keeps ever lengthening as in a melody where
everything is becoming but where the becoming, being itself
substantial, has no need of support. No more inert states, no
more dead things; nothing but the mobility of which the
stability of life is made. A vision of this kind, where reality
appears as continuous and indivisible, is on the road which
leads to philosophical intuition. . . .

If this knowledge is generalized, speculation will not be
the only thing to profit by it. Everyday life can be nourished
and illuminated by it. For the world into which our senses
and consciousness habitually introduce us is no more than
the shadow of itself: and it is as cold as death. Everything in
it is arranged for our maximum convenience, but in it, everything is in a present which seems constantly to be starting
afresh; and we ourselves, fashioned artificially in the image
of a no less artificial universe, see ourselves in the instantane-

ous, speak of the past as of something done away with, and see in memory a fact strange or in any case foreign to us, an aid given to mind by matter. Let us on the contrary grasp ourselves afresh as we are, in a present which is thick, and furthermore, elastic, which we can stretch indefinitely backward by pushing the screen which masks us from ourselves farther and farther away; let us grasp afresh the external world as it really is, not superficially, in the present, but in depth, with the immediate past crowding upon it and imprinting upon it its impetus; let us in a word become accustomed to see all things *sub specie durationis:* immediately in our galvanized perception what is taut becomes relaxed, what is dormant awakens, what is dead comes to life again. Satisfactions which art will never give save to those favored by nature and fortune, and only then upon rare occasions, philosophy thus understood will offer to all of us, at all times, by breathing life once again into the phantoms which surround us and by revivifying us. In so doing philosophy will become complementary to science in practice as well as in speculation. With its applications which aim only at the convenience of existence, science gives us the promise of well-being, or at most, of pleasure. But philosophy could already give us joy.

MIND—ENERGY [1]

Translated by H. WILDON CARR

LIFE AND CONSCIOUSNESS

. . . Philosophers who have speculated on the meaning of
life and on the destiny of man have failed to take sufficient
notice of an indication which nature itself has given us. Nature warns us by a clear sign that our destination is attained.
That sign is joy. I mean joy, not pleasure. Pleasure is only a
contrivance devised by nature to obtain for the creature the
preservation of its life, it does not indicate the direction in
which life is thrusting. But joy always announces that life has
succeeded, gained ground, conquered. All great joy has a
triumphant note. Now, if we take this indication into account and follow this new line of facts, we find that wherever
there is joy, there is creation; the richer the creation, the
deeper the joy. The mother beholding her child is joyous,
because she is conscious of having created it, physically and
morally. The merchant developing his business, the manu-
facturer seeing his industry prosper, are joyous,—is it because
money is gained and notoriety acquired? No doubt, riches
and social position count for much, but it is pleasures rather
than joy that they bring; true joy, here, is the feeling of having

[1] L'Energie spirituelle is a collection of lectures and essays which appeared in 1919. These excerpts are from Henri Bergson, Mind-Energy, trans.
by H. Wildon Carr. Copyright, 1920, by Henry Holt and Company, Inc.
Copyright, 1948, by H. Wildon Carr. Pp. 29–34, 68–74.

started an enterprise which goes, of having brought something to life. Take exceptional joys,—the joy of the artist who has realized his thought, the joy of the thinker who has made a discovery or invention. You may hear it said that these men work for glory and get their highest joy from the admiration they win. Profound error! We cling to praise and honors in the exact degree in which we are not sure of having succeeded. There is a touch of modesty in vanity. It is to reassure ourselves that we seek approbation; and just as we wrap the prematurely born child in cotton wool, so we gather round our work the warm admiration of mankind in case there should be insufficient vitality. But he who is sure, absolutely sure, of having produced a work which will endure and live, cares no more for praise and feels above glory, because he is a creator, because he knows it, because the joy he feels is the joy of a god. If, then, in every domain the triumph of life is creation, must we not suppose that human life has its goal in a creation which, unlike that of the artist and philosopher, can be pursued always by all men—creation of self by self, the growing of the personality by an effort which draws much from little, something from nothing, and adds unceasingly to whatever wealth the world contains?

Regarded from without, nature appears an immense inflorescence of unforeseeable novelty. The force which animates it seems to create lovingly, for nothing, for the mere pleasure of it, the endless variety of vegetable and animal species. On each it confers the absolute value of a great work of art. It seems as much attached to the first comer as to man himself. But the form of a living being, once designed, is thence-forward indefinitely repeated, and the acts of this living being, once performed, tend to imitate themselves and recommence automatically. Automatism and repetition, which prevail everywhere except in man, should warn us that living forms are only halts: this work of marking time is not the forward movement of life. The artist's standpoint is therefore important, but not final. Richness and originality of forms do indeed indicate an expansion of life, but in this expansion, where beauty means power, life also shows a stop of its impulse, a momentary powerlessness to push farther, like the boy who rounds off in a graceful curve the end of the slide.

The standpoint of the moralist is higher. In man alone, especially among the best of mankind, the vital movement pursues its way without hindrance, thrusting through that work of art, the human body, which it has created on its way, the creative current of the moral life. Man, called on at every moment to lean on the totality of his past in order to bring his weight to bear more effectively on the future, is the great success of life. But it is the moral man who is a creator in the highest degree,—the man whose action, itself intense, is also capable of intensifying the action of other men, and, itself generous, can kindle fires on the hearths of generosity. The men of moral grandeur, particularly those whose inventive and simple heroism has opened new paths to virtue, are re-vealers of metaphysical truth. Although they are the cul-minating point of evolution, yet they are nearest the source and they enable us to perceive the impulsion which comes from the deep. It is in studying these great lives, in striving to experience sympathetically what they experience, that we may penetrate by an act of intuition to the life principle itself. To pierce the mystery of the deep, it is sometimes necessary to regard the heights. It is earth's hidden fire which appears at the summit of the volcano.

On the two great routes that the vital impulse has found open before it, along the series of the arthropods and the series of the vertebrates, instinct and intelligence, at first wrapped up confusedly within one another, have in their development taken divergent directions. At the culminating point of the first evolution are the Hymenoptera, at the culminating point of the second, man. In each, in spite of the radical difference in the forms attained and the growing separation of the paths followed, it is to social life that evolution leads, as though the need of it was felt from the beginning, or rather as though there were some original and essential aspiration of life which could find full satisfaction only in society. Society, which is the community of individual energies, benefits from the efforts of all its members and renders effort easier to all. It can only subsist by subordinating the individual, it can only progress by leaving the individual free: contradictory requirements, which have to be reconciled. With insects, the first condition alone is fulfilled. The societies of ants and bees are admirably disciplined and united, but fixed in an invariable routine. If the individual is forgotten in the society, the society on its part also has forgotten its destination. Individual and society, both in a state of somnambulism, go round and round in the same circle, instead of moving straight forward to a greater social efficiency and a completer individual freedom. Human societies, alone, have kept full in view both the ends to be attained. Struggling among themselves and at war with one another, they are seeking clearly, by friction and shock, to round off the angles, to wear out antagonisms, to eliminate contradictions, to bring about that individual wills should insert themselves in the social will without losing their individual form, and that different and diverse societies should enter in their turn into a wider and more inclusive society and yet not lose their originality or their independence. The spectacle is both disquieting and reassuring, for we cannot contemplate it without saying that, here too, across innumerable obstacles,

life is working both by individualization and integration to
obtain the greatest quantity, the richest variety, the highest
qualities, of invention and effort. . . .

THE SOUL AND THE BODY

. . . But if the recollection has not been stored by the brain,
where then has it been preserved? Strictly speaking, I am
not sure that the question "where" can have a meaning when
we ask of it something different from a body. Sensitive plates
are stored in a box, phonographic rolls in cases; but why
should recollections, which are neither visible nor tangible,
need a container, and how could they have one? I will however accept, if you insist, but in a purely metaphorical sense,
the idea of a container in which recollections are lodged, and
I say then quite frankly they are in the mind. I make no hypothesis, I do not call in aid a mysterious entity, I confine
myself to observation. For there is nothing more immediately
given, nothing more evidently real, than consciousness, and
mind *is* consciousness. Now, consciousness signifies, before
everything, memory. At this moment that I am conversing
with you, I pronounce the word "conversation." Clearly my
consciousness presents the word all at once, otherwise it
would not be a whole word, and would not convey a single
meaning. Yet, when I pronounce the last syllable of the word,
the three first have already been pronounced; they are past
with regard to the last one, which must then be called the
present. But I did not pronounce this last syllable "tion" in-
stantaneously. The time, however short, during which I
uttered it is decomposable into parts, and all of these parts
are past in relation to the last among them. This last would
be the definitive present, were it not, in its turn, decomposable. So that, however you try, you cannot draw a line between the past and the present, nor consequently between

memory and consciousness. To make the brain the depository of the past, to imagine in the brain a certain region in which the past, once past, dwells, is to commit a psychological error, to attribute a scientific value to a distinction entirely practical, for there is no exact moment when the present becomes the past, nor consequently when perception becomes recollection. As a matter of fact, when I pronounce the word "conversation," there is present in my mind not only the beginning, the middle, and the end of the word, but also the words which preceded it and all the beginning of the sentence; otherwise I should have lost the thread of my speech. Now, if the punctuation of my speech had been different, my sentence might have begun sooner; it might, for example, have embraced all the preceding sentence, and my "present" would have been still more extended into the past. Push the argument to its limit, suppose that my speech had been lasting for years, since the first awakening of my consciousness, that it had been carried on in one single sentence, and that my consciousness were sufficiently detached from the future, disinterested enough in action, to be able to employ itself entirely in embracing the total meaning of the sentence: then I should no more seek the explanation of the integral preservation of this entire past than I seek the explanation of the preservation of the first three syllables of "conversation" when I pronounce the last syllable. Well, I believe that our whole psychical existence is something just like this single sentence, continued since the first awakening of consciousness, interspersed with commas, but never broken by full stops. And consequently I believe that our whole past still exists. It exists subconsciously, by which I mean that it is present to consciousness in such a manner that, to have the revelation of it, consciousness has no need to go out of itself or seek for foreign assistance; it has but to remove an obstacle, to withdraw a veil, in order that all that it contains, all in fact that it actually is, may be revealed. Fortunate are we to have this obstacle, infinitely precious to us is the veil! The brain is what secures to us this advantage. It keeps our attention fixed on life; and life looks forward; it looks back only in the degree to which the past can aid it to illumine and prepare the future. To live is, for the mind, essentially to concentrate itself on the action to be accomplished. To live is to be inserted in things by means of a mechanism which draws from consciousness all that is utilizable in action, all that can be acted on the stage, and darkens the greater part of the rest. Such is the brain's part in the work of memory: it does not serve to preserve the past, but primarily to mask it, then to allow only what is practically useful to emerge through the mask. Such, too, is the part the brain plays in regard to the mind generally. Extracting from the mind what is externalizable in movement, inserting the mind into this motor frame, it causes it to limit its vision, but also it makes its action efficacious. This means that the mind overflows the brain on all sides, and that cerebral activity responds only to a very small part of mental activity.

But this also means that mental life cannot be an effect of bodily life, that it looks much more as if the body were simply made use of by the mind, and that we have, therefore, no reason to suppose the body and the mind united inseparably to one another. I should not think of attacking, during the few minutes that are left to us, the most formidable problem that humanity can face. But still less should I think of stealing away from it. Whence do we come? What are we doing here? Whither are we bound? If philosophy could really offer no answer to these questions of vital interest, if it were incapable of gradually elucidating them as we elucidate problems of biology or history, if it were unable to forward the

study of them through an experience ever more profound
and a vision of reality ever more piercing, if it were bound
to be nothing better than an endless tournament between
those who affirm and those who deny immortality by de-
ductions from the hypothetical essence of the soul or of the
body, we could well indeed say,—to adopt a phrase of Pascal,
—that the whole of philosophy is not worth an hour's trouble.
True, immortality cannot indeed be proved experimentally,
for experience can only be experience of a limited duration;
and when religion speaks of immortality, it appeals to revelation. But it would be something, it would indeed be a great
step forward, were we able to establish on the ground of experience the possibility, much more were it the probability,
of survival for a time. The question whether this time is
finite or infinite could be left outside the domain of philosophy. Well, reduced to these modest proportions, the philosophic problem of the destiny of the soul does not seem to me
in the least insoluble. Here is a brain which works; and here
is a consciousness which feels, thinks and wills. If the work
of the brain corresponded to the totality of the consciousness,
if there were equivalence between the cerebral and the mental, consciousness might be bound up with the destiny of the
brain and death might be the end of all. Experience, at any
rate, would not speak to the contrary, and the philosopher
who affirms survival would then have to support his theory
by some metaphysical construction—usually a fragile thing.
But if, as I have tried to show, the mental life overflows the
cerebral life, if the brain does but translate into movements
a small part of what takes place in consciousness, then survival becomes so probable that the onus of proof falls on
him who denies it rather than on him who affirms it; for the
only reason we can have for believing in the extinction of
consciousness at death is that we see the body become dis-

organized, that this is a fact of experience, and the reason loses its force if the independence of almost the whole of consciousness with regard to the body has been shown to be also a fact of experience. In thus treating the problem of survival, in bringing it down from the heights on which traditional metaphysics has placed it, in transporting it into the field of experience, we are no doubt renouncing the immediate finding of a complete and radical solution. But what should we do? We have to choose, in philosophy, between the method of pure reasoning, which aims at a complete and decisive result, unable to be perfected since it is supposed to be perfect, and an empirical method, content with approximate results which can be endlessly corrected and enlarged. The first method, because it aims at making us immediately certain, condemns us to remain always in the simply probable or rather in the purely possible, for it is rare that it cannot serve to demonstrate indifferently either of two opposed theories equally coherent and equally plausible. The second aims first at simple probability, but since it works on a plane where probability may increase indefinitely, it brings us gradually to a state practically equivalent to certainty. Between these two ways of philosophizing I have long since made my choice. . . .

METAPHYSICS AND SCIENCE [1]

Translated by Mabelle L. Andison

To metaphysics, then, we assign a limited object, principally spirit, and a special method, mainly intuition. In doing this we make a clear distinction between metaphysics and science. But at the same time we attribute an equal value to both. I believe that they can both touch the bottom of reality. I reject the arguments advanced by philosophers, and accepted by scholars, on the relativity of knowledge and the impossibility of attaining the absolute.

Positive science, as a matter of fact, goes to sensible observation to obtain materials whose elaboration it entrusts to the faculty of abstracting and generalizing, to judgment and reasoning, to the intelligence. Having started from pure mathematics, it continued through mechanics, then through physics and chemistry; it arrived somewhat late in the day at biology. Its original domain, which has continued to be its preferred domain, is that of inert matter. It is less at its ease in the organized world, where it treads its way with an assured step only if it relies upon physics and chemistry; it clings to the physico-chemical in vital phenomena rather than

[1] From the second of two introductory chapters written for the collection of essays and lectures published in 1934 as *La Pensée et le Mouvant* and translated as *The Creative Mind* by Mabelle L. Andison. (New York, The Philosophical Library, 1946). This selection is on pages 42–52 with a long note that is on pages 301–303.

to what is really vital in the living. But great is its embarrassment when it reaches the mind. That does not mean that it cannot obtain some knowledge of it; but this knowledge becomes all the more vague the farther it gets away from the common borderline between mind and matter. One will never advance on this new terrain as on the old, relying solely on the power of logic. One must ceaselessly appeal from the *esprit géométrique* to the *esprit de finesse:* still, there is always something metaphorical in the formulas, however abstract, at which one arrives; as though the intelligence were obliged to transpose the psychic into the physical in order to understand and explain it. On the contrary, as soon as it comes back to inert matter, the science which arises from pure intelligence finds itself at home. This is in no way surprising. Our intelligence is the prolongation of our senses. Before we speculate we must live, and life demands that we make use of matter, either with our organs, which are natural tools, or with tools, properly so-called, which are artificial organs. Long before there was a philosophy and a science, the rôle of the intelligence was already that of manufacturing instruments and guiding the action of our body on surrounding bodies. Science has pushed this labor of the intelligence much further, but has not changed its direction. It aims above all at making us masters of matter. Even when science is speculating, it is still devoting its attention to acting, the value of scientific theories being gauged constantly by the solidity of the grip they give us on reality. But is that not precisely what should inspire us with complete confidence in positive science and also in the intelligence, its instrument? If the intellect has been made in order to utilize matter, its structure has no doubt been modelled upon that of matter. At least that is the simplest and most probable hypothesis. We should keep to it as long as it is not demonstrated to us that the intelligence deforms, transforms, constructs its object, or only brushes the surface, or grasps the mere semblance of it. Now nothing has ever been invoked by way of that demonstration, but the insoluble difficulties into which philosophy falls, the self-contradiction into which the intellect can fall when it speculates upon things as a whole—difficulties and contradictions we naturally come up against if the intellect is especially destined for the study of a part, and if we nevertheless mean to use it in knowing the whole. But it is not enough to say that. It is impossible to consider the mechanism of our intellect and the progress of our science without arriving at the conclusion that between intellect and matter there is, in fact, symmetry, concord and agreement. On the one hand, matter resolves itself more and more, in the eyes of the scholar, into mathematical relations, and on the other hand, the essential faculties of our intellect function with an absolute precision only when they are applied to geometry.

Doubtless, it might have been possible for mathematical science not to take originally the form the Greeks gave it. No doubt it must also, whatever form it adopts, keep to a strict use of artificial signs. But prior to this formulated mathematics, which is in large measure made up of convention, there is another, virtual or implicit, which is natural to the human mind. If the necessity of working with certain symbols makes the approach to mathematics difficult for many of us, the mind, in compensation, as soon as it has surmounted the obstacle, moves in this domain with a facility it has nowhere else, evidence being in this case immediate and theoretically instantaneous, the effort to understand existing most often in fact but not in right. In any other order of study, on the contrary, there must be, for understanding, a maturation process of thought which in some way adheres to the result, essentially fills up duration, and cannot even theoretically be conceived as instantaneous. In short, we might believe in a divergence between matter and intellect if we were to consider in matter only the superficial impressions made upon our senses, and if we were to leave to our intellect the vague and hazy form it takes in its daily operations. But when we bring the intellect back to its precise contours and when we delve deeply enough into our sense impressions so that matter begins to surrender to us its inner structure, we find that the articulations of the intellect apply exactly to those of matter. I therefore do not see why the science of matter should not reach an absolute. It instinctively assumes this scope, and all natural belief should be held as true, all appearance taken for reality, as long as its illusory character has not been established. Upon those who declare our science to be relative, upon those who claim that our knowledge deforms or constructs its object, now falls the burden of proof. And they cannot fulfill this obligation, for there is no room for the doctrine of the relativity of science when science and metaphysics are on their true ground, that to which we restore them.[1]

We recognize, furthermore, that the limits within which the intellect works have a certain elasticity, its contours a certain haziness, and that its indecision is exactly what permits it to be applied in some degree to the things of the mind. Matter and mind have this in common, that certain superficial agitations of matter are expressed in our minds, superficially, in the form of sensations; and on the other hand, the mind, in order to act upon the body, must descend little by little toward matter and become spatialized. It follows that the intelligence, although turned toward external things,

[1] Bergson here adds a note on Einstein's Theory of Relativity, which because of its length is printed separately at the end of this selection.

can still be exerted on things internal, provided that it does not claim to plunge too deeply.

But the temptation is great to carry to the very depth of the mind the application of those procedures which are successful as long as one remains near the surface. If one gives in to it, one will obtain purely and simply a physics of the mind traced upon that of bodies. Together these two physics will constitute a complete system of reality, what is sometimes called a metaphysics. How can one help but see that metaphysics thus understood fails to recognize the strictly spiritual in the mind, being only the extension to mind of what belongs to matter? And how can we help but see that in order to make this extension possible, we have had to take intellectual forms in a state of imprecision which still leaves them applicable to the superficial phenomena of the soul, and thereby condemns them to keeping less closely to the facts of the external world? Is it surprising that such a metaphysics, embracing both matter and mind at the same time, should give the effect of knowledge which is almost empty and in any case vague,—almost empty on the side of mind, since it has been able effectively to retain only superficial aspects of the soul, systematically vague on the side of matter, because the intelligence of the metaphysician must have sufficiently loosened its mechanism, and given it sufficient play to enable it to work equally well at the surface of matter or the surface of mind?

Quite different is the metaphysics that we place side by side with science. Granting to science the power of explaining matter by the mere force of intelligence, it reserves mind for itself. In this realm, proper to itself, it seeks to develop new functions of thought. Everyone can have noticed that it is more difficult to make progress in the knowledge of oneself than in the knowledge of the external world. Outside

oneself, the effort to learn is natural; one makes it with increasing facility; one applies rules. Within, attention must
remain tense and progress become more and more painful;
it is as though one were going against the natural bent. Is
there not something surprising in this? We are internal to
ourselves, and our personality is what we should know best.

Yet such is not the case; our mind is as if it were in a
strange land, whereas matter is familiar to it and in it the
mind is at home. But that is because a certain ignorance of
self is perhaps useful to a being which must exteriorize itself
in order to act; it answers a necessity of life. Our action is
exerted upon matter, and the farther the knowledge of matter
has been pursued the more efficacious is the action. It is doubtless to one's advantage, if one is to act effectively, to think of
what one will do, to understand what one has done, to have
a clear conception of what one might have done: nature
invites us to do so; it is one of the traits which distinguishes
man from the animal, completely intent as it is on the impression of the moment. But nature asks of us only a quick
glance at our inner selves; we then perceive the mind, but
the mind preparing to shape matter, already adapting itself
to it, assuming something of the spatial, the geometric, the
intellectual. A knowledge of the mind, in so far as it is
properly spiritual, would rather keep us from that end. We
draw nearer to it, on the contrary, when we study the structure of things. Thus nature turns mind away from mind,
turns mind toward matter. But in that way we see how we
can, if we like, indefinitely widen, deepen, and intensify the
vision of the mind which has been granted us. Since the insufficiency of this vision is due in the first place to the fact
that it is directed upon the mind already "spatialized" and
divided into mental compartments where matter can be inserted, let us separate the mind from the space in which it

is so at home, from the materiality which it takes to itself in order to rest upon matter. In so doing we shall restore it to itself and be able to comprehend it immediately. This direct vision of the mind by the mind is the chief function of intuition, as I understand it.

Intuition will be communicated only by the intelligence. It is more than idea; nevertheless in order to be transmitted, it will have to use ideas as a conveyance. It will prefer, however, to have recourse to the most concrete ideas, but those which still retain an outer fringe of images. Comparisons and metaphors will here suggest what cannot be expressed. That will not constitute a detour; it will amount to going straight to the goal. If one were constantly to speak an abstract, so-called "scientific" language, one would be giving of mind only its imitation by matter, for abstract ideas have been drawn from the external world and always imply a spatial representation: and yet one would think one had analyzed mind. Abstract ideas alone would, therefore, in such a case, be inviting us to imagine mind on the model of matter and to think it by transposition, that is, in the exact meaning of the word, by metaphor. Let us not be duped by appearances: there are cases in which it is imagery in language which knowingly expresses the literal meaning, and abstract language which unconsciously expresses itself figuratively. The moment we reach the spiritual world, the image, if it merely seeks to suggest, may give us the direct vision, while the abstract term, which is spatial in origin and which claims to express, most frequently leaves us in metaphor.

To sum it all up, what is wanted is a difference in method between metaphysics and science: I do not acknowledge a difference in value between the two. Less modest in my claims for science than most scholars have been, I consider that a science founded on experience as the moderns understand it, can attain the essence of the real. No doubt it embraces no more than a part of reality; but some day it will reach the bottom of that part; in any case, it will approach it indefinitely. It is, therefore, already fulfilling half of the program of the old metaphysics: it could be called metaphysics did it not prefer to keep the name of science. There remains the other half. This half seems to me to get back by right to a metaphysics which also starts from experience, and which, too, is itself capable of attaining the absolute: we should call it science, did not science prefer to limit itself to the other part of reality. Metaphysics, then, is not the superior of positive science; it does not come, after science, to consider the same object in order to obtain a higher knowledge of it. To suppose such a connection between them, as is the almost invariable custom among philosophers, is to wrong both of them: science, which one condemns to relativity; metaphysics, which will never be anything more than a hypothetical and vague knowledge, since science will necessarily have taken to itself in advance everything precise and certain that can be known of its object. Quite different is the relation I establish between metaphysics and science. It is my belief that they are, or that they can become, equally precise and certain. They both bear upon reality itself. But each one of them retains only half of it so that one might see in them, if one wished, two subdivisions of science or two departments of metaphysics, if they did not mark divergent directions of the activity of thought.

Precisely because they are on the same level, they have points in common and each one can, upon these points, be verified by the other. To establish between metaphysics and science a difference in dignity, to assign to them the same object, that is to say, the totality of things, stipulating that the one shall look at them from below and the other from above, is to exclude this mutual aid and reciprocal verification: in that case, metaphysics is, of necessity,—unless it loses all contact with the real—a condensed extract or hypothetical extension of science. Instead of this, let us allot to them different objects; to science let us leave matter, and to metaphysics, mind: as mind and matter touch one another, metaphysics and science, all along their common surface, will be able to test one another, until contact becomes fecundation. The results obtained on either side will of necessity be linked, because matter links up with mind. If the insertion is not perfect, it will be because there is something to rectify in our science, or in our metaphysics, or in both. Metaphysics will thus, by its peripheral part, exert a salutary influence upon science. Conversely, science will communicate to metaphysics habits of precision which will spread through it from the periphery to the centre. If only because its extremities will have to fit exactly upon those of positive science, our metaphysics will be that of the world in which we live, and not of all possible worlds. It will embrace realities.

That is to say that science and metaphysics will differ in object and method, but will commune in experience. Both of them will have put away the vague knowledge stored up in the usual concepts and transmitted by means of words. After all, what were we asking for metaphysics that had not already been obtained for science? For a long time the road had been barred to positive science by the claim made of reconstituting reality with the concepts set down in language. The "low" and the "high," the "heavy" and the "light," the "dry" and the "moist" were the elements one used in explaining the phenomena of nature; concepts were weighed, measured out and combined: it was an intellectual chemistry instead of physics. When it brushed concepts aside in order to look at things, even science seemed to revolt against intelligence; the "intellectualism" of that time recombined the material object, *a priori,* with elementary ideas. In reality, this science became more intellectualist than the inadequate physics which it replaced. It was obliged to become so, seeing that it was true, for matter and intellect are modelled upon one another, and in a science which reveals the exact configuration of matter our intellect necessarily finds its own image. The mathematical form which physics has taken is thus, at one and the same time, what best corresponds to reality and what is most satisfying to our understanding. Much less convenient will be the position of the true metaphysics. It also will begin by eliminating ready-made concepts; it also will rely upon experience. But that inner experience of which we speak will nowhere find a strictly appropriate language. It will of course be compelled to return to the concept, with at most the addition of the image; but then it will have to enlarge the concept, make it more flexible, and indicate, by the colored shading around the edge, that it does not contain the whole of experience. It is none the less true that metaphysics will have accomplished in its domain the reform that modern physics has brought about in its own. . . .

NOTE ON RELATIVITY [1]

It goes without saying that the relativity I am discussing here in order to exclude it from science taken at its limit, that is to say, to get rid of an error as it bears on the direction of scientific progress, has nothing to do with Einstein's relativity. His method consists essentially in finding a mathematical representation of things which will be independent of the observer's point of view (or, more precisely, of the system of

---

[1] See note 1 on page 125. This explanation by Bergson of the relationship between his thought and Einstein's is in *The Creative Mind,* pp. 301–303.

reference), and which consequently makes up a whole of *absolute relations*. Nothing is more contrary to relativity as philosophers understand it when they treat as relative our knowledge of the external world. The expression, "Theory of Relativity," unfortunately suggests to philosophers the opposite of what I am trying to express here.

Let me add, while on this subject of the Theory of Relativity, that it could not be appealed to either as supporting or confuting the metaphysics propounded in my various works, a metaphysics which has as its basis the experience of duration, along with the constatation of a certain connection between this duration and the space employed to measure it. To state a problem, the physicist whether relativist or no, takes his measurements in the Time here-now, which is our time and everybody else's. If he solves the problem, it is in the same Time, in this generalized Time, that he checks his solution. As for Time joined to Space, the fourth dimension of a Space-Time, it only exists within the interval between the posing of the problem and its solution, that is, within the equations, that is, on paper. This by no means detracts from the capital importance of the relativist conception by reason of its contribution to mathematical physics. But the reality of its Space-Time is purely mathematical, and one could not raise it to a metaphysical reality, or simply to "reality," without assigning to this last word a new meaning.

This term is most often applied to what is given in experience, or to what could be given—the real is what is verified or verifiable. Now, it is of the essence of Space-Time that it be unperceivable. One could not be put into it or put oneself in it, since the system of reference adopted is, by definition, a stationary system. Space and Time being distinct in it, and the physicist, actually existing and taking actual measurements, is he who occupies this system: all the other physicists, supposedly adopting other systems, are for him only imaginary physicists. I have already devoted a book to the demonstration of these various points.

I cannot resume it in a simple note. But as the book has often been misunderstood, I think it advisable to reproduce here the relevant passage of an article in which I accounted for this misunderstanding. Here indeed, is the point which ordinarily escapes those who, transferring themselves from physics to metaphysics, raise into reality—into things perceived or perceivable and existing before and after the calculation—a fusion of Space and Time which exists only in the calculation and which, outside it, renounces its essence the very moment existence is claimed for it.

In the hypothesis of Relativity, I said, it would be necessary to begin by seeing clearly why it is impossible to attach at the same time to several different systems "living and conscious" observers, why one single system—that which is effectively adopted as system of reference—contains real physicists, and why in particular the distinction between real physicists and physicists presumed real takes on a capital importance in the philosophic interpretation of this theory, when up to now philosophy had not had to concern itself with this theory in the interpretation of physics. The reason for this is nevertheless very simple.

From the point of view of Newtonian physics, for example, there is an absolutely privileged system of reference, an absolute rest and absolute motions. The universe is composed, at every instant, of material points of which some are motionless and others animated by movements perfectly determined. This universe is found to have within itself, in Space and Time, a concrete figure not depending on the point of view at which the physicist is placed: all physicists, whatever the mobile system to which they belong, refer in thought to the privileged system of reference and attribute to the universe the figure one would find in it on perceiving it thus in the absolute. If, then, the physicist *par excellence* is he who inhabits the privileged system, there is no call for establishing a radical distinction between this physicist and the others, since the others proceed as if they were in his place.

But in the Theory of Relativity, there is no longer a privileged system. All systems obtain. Any one of them can be chosen henceforth as system of reference, be "immobilized." In respect to this system of reference all the material points of the universe will still be found, some of them motionless, others animated by determined movements; but it will only be in relation to this system. Adopt another: the immobile will move, the moving will become motionless or alter its speed; the concrete figure of the universe will have radically changed. Yet the universe cannot present for you these two figures at the same time; the same material point cannot be imagined by you, or conceived, at once motionless and in motion. One must choose, and the moment you have chosen such and such determined figure you raise up as a living and conscious physicist, really perceiving, the physicist attached to the system of reference from which the universe takes this figure: the other physicists such as they appear in the figure of the universe thus chosen, are then virtual physicists, simply conceived as physicists by the real physicist. If you confer on one of them (as physicist) a reality, if you suppose him perceiving, acting, measuring, then his system is no longer a virtual system of reference, no longer simply conceived as being able to become a real system, but truly a real system of reference: it is then stationary, you have to do with a new figure of the world; and the real physicist just mentioned is now only a represented physicist.

M. Langevin stated definitively the essence of the Theory

of Relativity when he wrote that "the principle of Relativity, in its restricted, as well as more general form, is basically only the assertion of the existence of an independent reality of systems of reference, being in motion as they relate to each other and reckoning from which we observe their changing perspective. This universe has laws to which the employment of coördinates enables one to give an analytical form independent of the system of reference, and although the individual coördinates of each event depend on it nevertheless it can be expressed in intrinsic terms, as geometry has done with space, thanks to the introduction of invariant elements and the constituting of an appropriate language." In other words, the universe of Relativity is a universe as real, as independent of our mind, existing as absolutely as that of Newton and of general mankind. Only, whereas for general mankind, and even more so for Newton, this universe is a collection of things (even if physics confines itself to the study of relations between things) Einstein's universe is nothing more than the mere sum-total of relations. The invariant elements now held constitutive of the reality are expressions in which parameters enter, which are anything you like them to be, which no more represent Time or Space than anything else, because it is the relation between them that alone exists in the eyes of science, because, if there are no longer things, if the universe is without shape, no longer is there Time or Space.

To re-establish things, and consequently Time and Space (as one necessarily does each time one wishes to be informed about a definite physical event, perceived in definite points of Space and Time), one is obliged to restore a shape to the world; but this will be to have chosen a point of view, to have adopted a system of reference. The system chosen becomes, moreover, by its very adoption, the central system.

The Theory of Relativity has precisely for its essence to guarantee to us that the mathematical expression of the world which we find from this arbitrarily chosen point of view will be identical, if we conform to the rules it has laid down, to that which we would have found in placing ourselves at any other point of view. Keep only this mathematical expression, and there is no more Time than there is anything else. Restore Time and you re-establish things, but you have chosen a system of reference and the physicist who is tied to it. For the moment there can be no other, though any other might have been chosen.

THE TWO SOURCES OF MORALITY AND RELIGION [1]

Translated by R. ASHLEY AUDRA and CLOUDESLEY BRERETON
with the assistance of W. HORSFALL CARTER

CLOSED AND OPEN SOCIETIES

. . . Let us consider two divergent lines of evolution with
societies at the extremities of each. The type of society which
will appear the more natural will obviously be the instinctive
type; the link that unites the bees of a hive resembles far
more the link which holds together the cells of an organism,
coördinate and subordinate to one another. Let us suppose for
an instant that nature has intended to produce at the extremity of the second line societies where a certain latitude was
left to individual choice: she would have arranged that intelligence should achieve here results comparable, as regards
their regularity, to those of instinct in the other; she would
have had recourse to habit. Each of these habits, which may
be called "moral," would be incidental. But the aggregate of
them, I mean the habit of contracting these habits, being at
the very basis of societies and a necessary condition of their
existence, would have a force comparable to that of instinct

[1] *Les Deux Sources de la Morale et de la Religion* first appeared in 1932.
This translation, supervised by the author, was made in 1935. These selec-
tions are from Henri Bergson, *The Two Sources of Morality and Religion*,
trans. by R. Ashley Audra and Cloudesley Brereton with the assistance of
W. Horsfall Carter. Copyright, 1935, by Henry Holt and Company, Inc.
Pp. 18–21, 25–32, 42–46, 193–194, and 217–223.

in respect of both intensity and regularity. This is exactly what we have called the "totality of obligation." This, be it said, will apply only to human societies at the moment of emerging from the hands of nature. It will apply to primitive and to elementary societies. But, however much human society may progress, grow complicated and spiritualized, the original design, expressing the purpose of nature, will remain.

Now this is exactly what has happened. Without going deeply into a matter we have dealt with elsewhere, let us simply say that intelligence and instinct are forms of consciousness which must have interpenetrated each other in their rudimentary state and become dissociated as they grew. This development occurred on the two main lines of evolution of animal life, with the Arthropods and the Vertebrates. At the end of the former we have the instinct of insects, more especially the Hymenoptera; at the end of the second, human intelligence. Instinct and intelligence have each as their essential object the utilization of implements: in the first case, organs supplied by nature and hence immutable; in the second, invented tools, and therefore varied and unforeseen. The implement is, moreover, designed for a certain type of work, and this work is all the more efficient the more it is specialized, the more it is divided up between diversely qualified workers who mutually supplement one another. Social life is thus immanent, like a vague ideal, in instinct as well as in intelligence: this ideal finds its most complete expression in the hive or the anthill on the one hand, in human societies on the other. Whether human or animal, a society is an organization; it implies a coördination and generally also a subordination of elements; it therefore exhibits, whether merely embodied in life or, in addition, specifically formulated, a collection of rules and laws. But in a hive or an anthill the individual is riveted to his task by his structure, and the organization is relatively invariable, whereas the human community is variable in form, open to every kind of progress. The result is that in the former each rule is laid down by nature, and is necessary: whereas in the latter only one thing is natural, the necessity of a rule. Thus the more, in human society, we delve down to the root of the various obligations to reach obligation in general, the more obligation will tend to become necessity, the nearer it will draw, in its peremptory aspect, to instinct. And yet we should make a great mistake if we tried to ascribe any particular obligation, whatever it might be, to instinct. What we must perpetually recall is that, no one obligation being instinctive, obligation as a whole *would have been* instinct if human societies were not, so to speak, ballasted with variability and intelligence. It is a virtual instinct, like that which lies behind the habit of speech. The morality of a human society may indeed be compared to its language. If ants exchange signs, which seems probable, those signs are provided by the very instinct that makes the ants communicate with one another. On the contrary, our languages are the product of custom. Nothing in the vocabulary, or even in the syntax, comes from nature. But speech is natural, and unvarying signs, natural in origin, which are presumably used in a community of insects, exhibit what our language would have been, if nature in bestowing on us the faculty of speech had not added that function which, since it makes and uses tools, is inventive and called intelligence. We must perpetually recur to what obligation *would have been* if human society had been instinctive instead of intelligent: this will not explain any particular obligation, we shall even give of obligation in general an idea which would be false, if if we went no further; and yet we must think of this instinctive society as the counterpart of intelligent society, if we are not to start without any clue in quest of the foundations of morality.

From this point of view obligation loses its specific character. It ranks among the most general phenomena of life. When the elements which go to make up an organism submit to a rigid discipline, can we say that they feel themselves liable to obligation and that they are obeying a social instinct? Obviously not; but whereas such an organism is barely a community, the hive and the anthill are actual organisms, the elements of which are united by invisible ties, and the social instinct of an ant—I mean the force by virtue of which the worker, for example, performs the task to which she is predestined by her structure—cannot differ radically from the cause, whatever it be, by virtue of which every tissue, every cell of a living body, toils for the greatest good of the whole. Indeed it is, strictly speaking, no more a matter of obligation in the one case than in the other, but rather of necessity. It is just this necessity that we perceive, not actual but virtual, at the foundations of moral obligation, as through a more or less transparent veil. A human being feels an obligation only if he is free, and each obligation, considered separately, implies liberty. But it is necessary that there should be obligations; and the deeper we go, away from those particular obligations which are at the top, towards obligation in general, or, as we have said, towards obligation as a whole, which is at the bottom, the more obligation appears as the very form assumed by necessity in the realm of life, when it demands, for the accomplishment of certain ends, intelligence, choice, and therefore liberty. . . .

OPEN SOULS

We have been searching for pure obligation. To find it we have had to reduce morality to its simplest expression. The

advantage of this has been to indicate in what obligation consisted; the disadvantage, to narrow down morality enormously. Not indeed because that part of it which we have
left on one side is not obligatory: is there such a thing as a
duty which is not compulsory? But it is conceivable that,
starting from a primitive basis of obligation pure and simple,
such as we have just defined, this obligation should radiate,
expand, and even come to be absorbed into something that
transfigures it. Let us now see what complete morality would
be like. We shall use the same method and once more proceed, not downwards as up to now but upwards, to the extreme limit.

In all times there have arisen exceptional men, incarnating
this morality. Before the saints of Christianity, mankind had
known the sages of Greece, the prophets of Israel, the Ara-
hats of Buddhism, and others besides. It is to them that
men have always turned for that complete morality which
we had best call absolute morality. And this very fact is at
once characteristic and instructive; this very fact suggests to
us the existence of a difference of kind and not merely one of
degree between the morality with which we have been dealing up to now and that we are about to study, between the
minimum and the maximum, between the two extremes.
Whereas the former is all the more unalloyed and perfect precisely in proportion as it is the more readily reduced to impersonal formulae, the second, in order to be fully itself, must
be incarnate in a privileged person who becomes an example.
The generality of the one consists in the universal acceptance
of a law, that of the other in a common imitation of a model.

Why is it, then, that saints have their imitators, and why
do the great moral leaders draw the masses after them? They
ask nothing, and yet they receive. They have no need to ex-
hort; their mere existence suffices. For such is precisely the

nature of this other morality. Whereas natural obligation is a pressure or a propulsive force, complete and perfect morality has the effect of an appeal.

Only those who have come into touch with a great moral personality have fully realized the nature of this appeal. But we all, at those momentous hours when our usual maxims of conduct strike us as inadequate, have wondered what such or such a one would have expected of us under the circumstances. It might have been a relation or a friend whom we thus evoked in thought. But it might quite as well have been a man we had never met, whose life-story had merely been told us, and to whose judgment we in imagination submitted our conduct, fearful of his censure, proud of his approval. It might even be a personality brought up from the depths of the soul into the light of consciousness, stirring into life within us, which we felt might completely pervade us later, and to which we wished to attach ourselves for the time being, as the disciple to his teacher. As a matter of fact this personality takes shape as soon as we adopt a model; the longing to resemble, which ideally generates the form, is an incipient resemblance; the word which we shall make our own is the word whose echo we have heard within ourselves. But the person matters little. Let us merely make the point that, whereas the first morality was the more potent the more distinctly it broke up into impersonal obligation, on the contrary the latter morality, at first dispersed among general precepts to which our intelligence gave its allegiance, but which did not go so far as to set our will in motion, becomes more and more cogent in proportion as the multiplicity and generality of its maxims merge more completely into a man's unity and individuality.

Whence does it derive its strength? What is the principle of action which here takes the place of the natural obligation, or rather which ends by absorbing it? To discover this, let us first see what is tacitly demanded of us. The duties dealt with so far are those imposed on us by social life; they are binding in respect of the city more than in respect of humanity. You might say that the second morality—if we *do* distinguish two—differs from the first in that it is human instead of being merely social. And you would not be entirely wrong. For we have seen that it is not by widening the bounds of the city that you reach humanity; between a social morality and a human morality the difference is not one of degree but of kind. The former is the one of which we are generally thinking when we feel a natural obligation. Superimposed upon these clearly defined duties we like to imagine others, the lines of which are perhaps a little blurred. Loyalty, sacrifice of self, the spirit of renunciation, charity, such are the words we use when we think of these things. But have we, generally speaking, in mind at such times anything more than words? Probably not, and we fully realize this. It is sufficient, we say, that the formula is there; it will take on its full meaning, the idea which is to fill it out will become operative, when the occasion arises. It is true that for many people the occasion will never arise or the action will be put off till later. With certain people the will does make a feeble start, but so feeble that the slight shock they feel can in fact be attributed to no more than the expansion of social duty broadened and weakened into human duty. But only let these formulae be invested with substance, and that substance become animate, lo and behold! a new life is proclaimed; we understand, we feel the advent of a new morality. Consequently, in speaking here of love of humanity we should doubtless be denoting this morality. And yet we should not be expressing the essence of it, for the love of humanity is not a self-sufficient force or one which has a direct efficacy. The teachers of the young know full well that you cannot prevail over egoism by recommending "altruism." It even happens that a generous nature, eager to sacrifice itself, experiences a sudden chill at the idea that it is working "for mankind." The object is too vast, the effect too diffuse. We may therefore conjecture that if a love of humanity constitutes this morality, it constitutes it in much the same way as the intention of reaching a certain point implies the necessity of crossing an intervening space. In one sense it is the same thing; in another sense it is something entirely different. If we think only of the interval and the various points, infinite in number, which we still have to pass one by one, we shall be discouraged from starting, like Zeno's arrow, and besides there would be no object, no inducement. But if we step across the intervening space, thinking only of the goal or looking even beyond it, we shall easily accomplish a simple act, and at the same time overcome the infinite multiplicity of which this simplicity is the equivalent. What then, in this case, is the goal, what the direction of the effort? What exactly, in a word, is required of us?

Let us first define the moral attitude of the man we have been considering up to now. He is part and parcel of society; he and it are absorbed together in the same task of individual and social preservation. Both are self-centered. True, it is doubtful whether private interest invariably agrees with public interest: we know against what insurmountable difficulties utilitarian ethics has always come up when it laid down the principle that the individual could seek only his own good, while maintaining that this would lead him to desire the good of others. An intelligent being, pursuing his personal advantage, will often do something quite different from what the general interest demands. Yet, if utilitarian ethics persists in recurring in one form or another, this means that it is not untenable, and if it is tenable the reason is precisely because, beneath the intelligent activity, forced in fact to choose between its own interests and those of others, there lies a substratum of instinctive activity, originally implanted there by nature, where the individual and the social are well-nigh indistinguishable. The cell lives for itself and also for the organism, imparting to it vitality and borrowing vitality from it; it will sacrifice itself to the whole, if need be; and it would doubtless then say, if it were conscious, that it made this sacrifice in its own interest. Such would probably be the state of mind of an ant reflecting on her conduct. She would feel that her activity hinges on something intermediate between the good of the ant and the good of the anthill. Now it is just with this fundamental instinct that we have associated obligation as such: it implies at the beginning a state of things in which the individual and society are not distinguishable. This is what enables us to say that the attitude to which it corresponds is that of an individual and a community concentrated on themselves. At once individual and social, the soul here moves round in a circle. It is closed.

The other attitude is that of the open soul. What, in that case, is allowed in? Suppose we say that it embraces all humanity: we should not be going too far, we should hardly be going far enough, since its love may extend to animals, to plants, to all nature. And yet no one of these things which would thus fill it would suffice to define the attitude taken by the soul, for it could, strictly speaking, do without all of them. Its form is not dependent on its content. We have just filled it; we could as easily empty it again. "Charity" would persist in him who possesses "charity," though there be no other living creature on earth.

Once again, it is not by a process of expansion of the self that we can pass from the first state to the second. A psychology which is too purely intellectualist, following the indications of speech, will doubtless define feelings by the things with which they are associated; love for one's family, love for one's country, love of mankind, it will see in these three inclinations one single feeling, growing ever larger, to embrace an increasing number of persons. The fact that these feelings are outwardly expressed by the same attitude or the same sort of motion, that all three *incline* us to something, enables us to group them under the concept "love," and to express them by one and the same word; we then distinguish them by naming three objects, each larger than the other, to which they are supposed to apply. This does in fact suffice to distinguish them. But does it describe them? Or analyze them? At a glance, consciousness perceives between the two first feelings and the third a difference of kind. The first imply a choice, therefore an exclusion; they may act as incentives to strife, they do not exclude hatred. The latter is all love. The former alight directly on an object which attracts them. The latter does not yield to the attraction of its object; it has not aimed at this object; it has shot beyond and reached humanity only by passing through humanity. Has it, strictly speaking, an object? We shall ask this question. But for the present we shall confine ourselves to noting that this psychic attitude, or rather psychic motion, is self-sufficient.

Nevertheless there arises in regard to it a problem which stands ready solved in the case of the other. For that other was ordained by nature; we have just seen how and why we feel bound to adopt it. But the second attitude is acquired; it calls for, has always called for, an effort. How comes it that the men who have set the example have found other men to follow them? And what is the power that is in this case the counterpart of social pressure? We have no choice. Beyond instinct and habit there is no direct action on the will except feeling. The impulse given by feeling can indeed closely resemble obligation. Analyze the passion of love, particularly in its early stages; is pleasure its aim? Could we not as well say it is pain? Perhaps a tragedy lies ahead, a whole life wrecked, wasted, ruined, we know it, we feel it, no matter, we must because we must. Indeed the worst perfidy of a nascent passion is that it counterfeits duty. But we need not go as far as passion. Into the most peaceful emotion there may enter a certain demand for action, which differs from obligation as described above in that it will meet with no resistance, in that it imposes only what has already been acquiesced in, but which none the less resembles obligation in that it does impose something. Nowhere do we see this more clearly than in those cases where the demand ceases to have any practical consequence, thus leaving us the leisure to reflect upon it and anlyze what we feel. This is what occurs in musical emotion, for example. We feel, while we listen, as though we could not desire anything else but what the music is suggesting to us, and that that is just as we should naturally and necessarily act did we not refrain from action to listen. Let the music express joy or grief, pity or love, every moment we are what it expresses. Not only ourselves, but many others, nay, all the others, too. When music weeps, all humanity, all nature, weeps with it. In point of fact it does not introduce these feelings into us; it introduces us into them, as passers-by are forced into a street dance. Thus do pioneers in morality proceed. Life holds for them unsuspected tones of feeling like those of some new symphony, and they draw us after them into this music that we may express it in action. . . .

THE GREAT MYSTICS

. . . the maxims of the second morality do not work singly like those of the first: as soon as one of them, ceasing to be abstract, becomes filled with significance and acquires the capacity to act, the others tend to do the same: at last they all fuse in the warm emotion which left them behind long ago, and in the men, now come to life again, who experienced it. Founders and reformers of religions, mystics and saints, obscure heroes of moral life whom we have met on our way and who are in our eyes the equals of the greatest, they are all there: inspired by their example, we follow them, as if we were joining an army of conquerors. They are indeed conquerors: they have broken down natural resistance and raised humanity to a new destiny. Thus, when we dispel appearances to get at reality, when we set aside the common form assumed, thanks to mutual exchanges, by the two moralities in conceptual thought and in speech, then, at the two extremes of the single morality we find pressure and aspiration: the former the more perfect as it becomes more impersonal, closer to these natural forces which we call habit or even instinct, the latter the more powerful according as it is more obviously aroused in us by definite persons, and the more it apparently triumphs over nature. True, if we went down to the roots of nature itself we should perhaps find that the same force which manifests itself directly, rotating on its own axis, in the human species once constituted, also acts later and indirectly, through the medium of privileged persons, in order to drive humanity forward.

But there is no need to resort to metaphysics to determine the relation between this pressure and this aspiration. Once again, there is some difficulty in comparing the two moralities because they are no longer to be found in a pure state. The first has handed on to the second something of its compulsive force; the second has diffused over the other something of its perfume. We find ourselves in the presence of a series of steps up or down, according as we range through the dictates of morality from one extreme or from the other; as to the two extreme limits, they have chiefly a theoretical interest; it is not often that they are actually attained. Let us, nevertheless, consider separately, in themselves, pressure and aspiration. Immanent in the former is the representation of a society which aims only at self-preservation; the circular movement in which it carries round with it individuals, as it revolves on the same spot, is a vague imitation, through the medium of habit, of the immobility of instinct. The feeling which would characterize the consciousness of these pure obligations, assuming they were all fulfilled, would be a state of individual and social well-being similar to that which accompanies the normal working of life. It would resemble pleasure rather than joy. The morality of aspiration, on the contrary, implicitly contains the feeling of progress. The emotion of which we were speaking is the enthusiasm of a forward movement, enthusiasm by means of which this morality has won over a few and has then, through them, spread over the world. "Progress" and "advance," moreover, are in this case indistinguishable from the enthusiasm itself. To become conscious of them it is not necessary that we should picture a goal that we are trying to reach or a perfection to which we are approximating. It is enough that the joy of enthusiasm involves something more than the pleasure of well-being: the pleasure not implying the joy, while the joy does imply and encompass the pleasure. We feel this to be so, and the certainty thus obtained, far from hinging on a metaphysical theory, is what will provide it with its firmest support.

But antecedent to this metaphysical theory, and far nearer to what we have directly experienced, are the simpler representations which in this case spring from the emotion in proportion as we dwell on it. We were speaking of the founders and reformers of religion, the mystics and the saints. Let us

hearken to their language; it merely expresses in representations the emotions peculiar to a soul opening out, breaking
with nature, which enclosed it both within itself, and within
the city.

They begin by saying that what they experience is a feeling
of liberation. Well-being, pleasures, riches, all those things
that mean so much to the common run of men, leave them indifferent. In breaking away from them they feel relief, and
then exhilaration. Not that nature was wrong in attaching
us by strong ties to the life she had ordained for us. But we
must go further, and the amenities which are real comforts
at home would become hindrances, burdensome impedi-
menta, if we had to take them on our travels. That a soul thus
equipped for action would be more drawn to sympathize
with other souls, and even with the whole of nature, might
surprise us, if the relative immobility of the soul, revolving in
a circle in an enclosed society, was not due precisely to the
fact that nature has split humanity into a variety of individuals by the very act which constituted the human species.
Like all acts creative of a species, this was a halt on the road.
By a resumption of the forward movement, the decision to
halt is broken. True, to obtain a complete effect, the privileged soul would have to carry the rest of humanity with it.
But if a few follow, and if the others imagine they would do
likewise on occasion, this already means a great deal, henceforth, with the beginning of accomplishment, there will be
the hope that the circle may be broken in the end. In any case,
we cannot repeat too often that it is not by preaching the love
of our neighbor that we can obtain it. It is not by expanding
our narrower feelings that we can embrace humanity. However much our intelligence may convince itself that this is
the line of advance, things behave differently. What is simple
for our understanding is not necessarily so for our will. In

cases where logic affirms that a certain road should be the
shortest, experience intervenes, and finds that in that direction there is no road. The truth is that heroism may be the
only way to love. Now, heroism cannot be preached, it has
only to show itself, and its mere presence may stir others to
action. For heroism itself is a return to movement, and ema-
nates from an emotion—infectious like all emotions—akin to
the creative act. Religion expresses this truth in its own way
by saying that it is in God that we love all other men. And all
great mystics declare that they have the impression of a current passing from their soul to God, and flowing back again
from God to mankind.

Let no one speak of material obstacles to a soul thus freed!
It will not answer that we can get round the obstacle, or
that we can break it; it will declare that there is no obstacle.
We cannot even say of this moral conviction that it moves
mountains, for it sees no mountains to move. So long as you
argue about the obstacle, it will stay where it is; and so long
as you look at it, you will divide it into parts which will have
to be overcome one by one; there may be no limit to their
number; perhaps you will never exhaust them. But you can
do away with the whole, at a stroke, if you deny its existence.
That is what the philosopher did who proved movement by
walking: his act was the negation pure and simple of the effort, perpetually to be renewed, and therefore fruitless, which
Zeno judged indispensable to cover, one by one, the stages of
the intervening space. By going deeply into this new aspect
of morality, we should find an impression of coincidence, real
or imaginary, with the generative effort of life. If seen from
outside, the activity of life lends itself, in each of its works, to
an analysis which might be carried on indefinitely; there is
no end to a description of the structure of an eye such as ours.
But what we call a series of means employed is, in reality, but

a number of obstacles overcome; the action of nature is simple, and the infinite complexity of the mechanism which it seems to have built up piece by piece to achieve the power of vision is but the endless network of opposing forces which have cancelled one another out to secure an uninterrupted channel for the functioning of the faculty. So, if we took into account only what we saw, the simple act of an invisible hand plunged into iron filings would seem like an inexhaustible interplay of actions and reactions among the filings themselves in order that they might effect an equilibrium. If such is the contrast between the real working of life and the aspect it presents to the senses and the intelligence which analyze it, is it surprising that a soul which no more recognizes any material obstacle should feel itself, rightly or wrongly, at one with the principle of life?

STATIC RELIGION

Man is the only animal whose actions are uncertain, who hesitates, gropes about and lays plans in the hope of success and the fear of failure. He is alone in realizing that he is subject to illness, alone in knowing that he must die. The rest of nature goes on its expanding course in absolute tranquillity. Although plants and animals are the sport of chance, they rely on the passing hour as they would on eternity. We drink in something of this unshakable confidence during a country walk, from which we return quieted and soothed. But this is not saying enough. Of all the creatures that live in society, man alone can swerve from the social line by giving way to selfish preoccupations when the common good is at stake; in all other societies the interests of the individual are inexorably coördinate with and subordinate to the general interest. This twofold shortcoming in man is the price paid for intelligence. Man cannot exert his faculty of thought without imagining an uncertain future, which rouses his fears and his hopes. He cannot think about what nature demands of him, in so far as she has made a social being of him, without saying to himself that he might often find it more profitable to ignore others and think of himself alone. In both cases there would be a break of the normal, natural order of things. And yet it was nature who ordained intelligence, who placed it at the end of one of the two great lines of evolution as a counterpart to the highest form of instinct, which is the terminal point of the other. It is impossible that she should not have taken the precaution to see that a condition of order, which had been even slightly disturbed by intelligence, should tend to re-establish itself automatically. As a matter of fact, the myth-making function, which belongs to intelligence, and which yet is not pure intelligence, has precisely this object. Its rôle is to elaborate that religion we have been dealing with up to now, that which we call static, and of which we should say that it was natural religion, if the term were not used in another sense. We have then only to sum up what we have said to define this religion in clear terms. *It is a defensive reaction of nature against what might be depressing for the individual, and dissolvent for society, in the exercise of intelligence.*

DYNAMIC RELIGION

When we grasp that such (superabundant activity) is the culminating point of the inner evolution of the great mystics, we can but wonder how they could ever have been classed with the mentally diseased. True, we live in a condition of unstable equilibrium; normal health of mind, as, indeed, of body, is not easily defined. Yet there is an exceptional, deep-rooted mental healthiness, which is readily recognizable. It is expressed in the bent for action, the faculty of adapting and re-adapting oneself to circumstances, in firmness combined with suppleness, in the prophetic discernment of what is possible and what is not, in the spirit of simplicity which triumphs over complications, in a word, supreme good sense. Is not this exactly what we find in the above-named mystics? (Saint Paul, Saint Teresa, Saint Catherine of Siena, Saint Francis, Joan of Arc.) And might they not provide us with the very definition of intellectual vigor?

If they have been judged otherwise, it is because of the abnormal states which are, with them, the prelude to the ultimate transformation. They talk of their visions, their ecstasies, their raptures. These are phenomena which also occur in sick people and which are part of their malady. An important work has lately appeared on ecstasy regarded as a psychoasthenic manifestation. (Pierre Janet, *De l'angoisse à l'extase.*) But there exist morbid states which are imitations of healthy states; the latter are none the less healthy, and the former morbid. A lunatic may think he is an emperor; he will systematically introduce a Napoleonic touch into his gestures, his words, his acts, and therein lies his madness: does it in any way reflect upon Napoleon? In just the same way it is possible to parody mysticism, and the result will be mystic insanity: does it follow that mysticism is insanity? Yet there is no denying that ecstasies, visions, raptures, are abnormal states, and that it is difficult to distinguish between the abnormal and the morbid. And such indeed has been the opinion of the great mystics themselves. They have been the first to warn their disciples against visions which were quite likely to be pure hallucinations. And they generally regarded their own visions, when they had any, as of secondary importance, as wayside incidents; they had had to go beyond them, leaving raptures and ecstasies far behind, to reach the goal, which was identification of the human will with the divine will.

The truth is that these abnormal states, resembling morbid states, and sometimes doubtless very much akin to them, are easily comprehensible, if we only stop to think what a shock to the soul is the passing from the static to the dynamic, from the closed to the open, from everyday life to mystic life. When the darkest depths of the soul are stirred, what rises to the surface and attains consciousness takes on there, if it be intense enough, the form of an image or an emotion. The image is often pure hallucination, just as the emotion may be meaningless agitation. But they both may express the fact that the disturbance is a systematic readjustment with a view to equilibrium on a higher level: the image then becomes symbolic of what is about to happen, and the emotion is a concentration of the soul awaiting transformation. The latter is the case of mysticism, but it may partake of the other; what is only abnormal may be accompanied by what is distinctly morbid; we cannot upset the regular relation of the conscious to the unconscious without running a risk. So we must not be surprised if nervous disturbances and mysticism sometimes go together; we find the same disturbances in other forms of genius, notably in musicians. They have to be regarded as merely accidental. The former have no more to do with mystical inspiration than the latter with musical.

Shaken to its depths by the current which is about to sweep it forward, the soul ceases to revolve round itself and escapes for a moment from the law which demands that the species and the individual should condition one another. It stops as though to listen to a voice calling. Then it lets itself go, straight onward. It does not directly perceive the force that moves it, but it feels an indefinable presence, or divines it through a symbolic vision. Then comes a boundless joy, an all-absorbing ecstasy or an enthralling rapture: God is there, and the soul is in God. Mystery is no more. Problems vanish, darkness is dispelled; everything is flooded with light. But for how long? An imperceptible anxiety, hovering above the ecstasy, descends and clings to it like its shadow. This anxiety alone would suffice, even without the phases which are to come, to distinguish true and complete mysticism from what was in bygone days its anticipated imitation or preparation. For it shows that the soul of the great mystic does not stop at ecstasy, as at the end of a journey. The ecstasy is indeed rest, if you like, but as though at a station, where the engine is still under steam, the onward movement becoming a vibration on one spot, until it is time to race forward again. Let us put it more clearly: however close the union with God may be, it could be final only if it were total. Gone, doubtless, is the distance between the thought and the object of the thought, since the problems which measured and indeed constituted the gap have disappeared. Gone the radical separation between him who loves and him who is beloved: God is there, and joy is boundless. But though the soul becomes, in thought and feeling, absorbed in God, something of it remains outside; that something is the will, whence the soul's action, if it acted, would quite naturally proceed. Its life, then, is not yet divine. The soul is aware of this, hence its vague disquietude, hence the agitation in repose which is the striking feature of what we call complete mysticism: it means that the impetus has acquired the momentum to go further, that ecstasy affects indeed the ability to see and to feel, but that there is, besides, the will, which itself has to find its way back to God. When this agitation has grown to the extent of displacing everything else, the ecstasy has died out, the soul finds itself alone again, and sometimes desolate. Accustomed for a time to a dazzling light, it is now left blindly groping in the gloom. It does not realize the profound metamorphosis which is going on obscurely within it. It feels that it has lost much; it does not yet know that this was in order to gain all. Such is the "darkest night" of which the great mystics have spoken, and which is perhaps the most significant thing, in any case the most instructive, in Christian mysticism. The final phase, characteristic of great mysticism, is imminent. To analyze this ultimate preparation is impossible, for the mystics themselves have barely had a glimpse of its mechanism. Let us confine ourselves to suggesting that a machine of wonderfully tempered steel, built for some extraordinary feat, might be in a somewhat similar state if it became conscious of itself as it was being put together. Its parts being one by one subjected to the severest tests, some of them rejected and replaced by others, it would have a feeling of something lacking here and there, and of pain all over. But this entirely superficial distress would only have to be intensified in order to pass into the hope and expectation of a marvelous instrument. The mystic soul yearns to become this instrument. It throws off anything in its substance that is not pure enough, not flexible and strong enough, to be turned to some use by God. Already it had sensed the presence of God, it had thought it beheld God in a symbolic vision, it had even been united to Him in its ecstasy; but none of this rapture was lasting, because it was mere contemplation; action threw the soul back upon itself and thus divorced it from God. *Now* it is God who is acting through the soul, in the soul; the union is total, therefore final. At this point words such as mechanism and instrument evoke images which are better left alone. They could be used to give us an idea of the preliminary work. They will teach us nothing of the final result. Let us say that henceforth for the soul there is a superabundance of life. There is a boundless impetus. There is an irresistible impulse which hurls it into vast enterprises. A calm exaltation of all its faculties makes it see things on a vast scale only, and, in spite of its own weakness, produce only what can be mightily wrought. Above all, it sees things simply, and this simplicity, which is equally striking in the words it uses and the conduct it follows, guides it through complications which it apparently does not even perceive. An innate knowledge, or rather an acquired ignorance, suggests to it straightaway the step to be taken, the decisive act, the unanswerable word. Yet effort remains indispensable, endurance and perseverance likewise. But they come of themselves, they develop of their own accord, in a soul acting and acted upon, whose liberty coincides with the divine activity. They represent a vast expenditure of energy, but this energy is supplied as it is required, for the superabundance of vitality which it demands flows from a spring which is the very source of life. And now the visions are left far behind: the divinity could not manifest itself from without to a soul henceforth replete with its essence. Nothing remains to distinguish such a man outwardly from the men about him. He alone realizes the change which has raised him to the rank of *adjutores Dei,* "patients" in respect to God, agents in respect to man. In this elevation he feels no pride. On the contrary, great is his humility. How could he be aught but humble, when there has been made manifest to him, in mute colloquy, alone with The Alone, through an emotion in which his whole soul seemed to be absorbed, what we may call the divine humility?

Even in the mysticism which went only as far as ecstasy, that is to say contemplation, a certain line of action was foreshadowed. Hardly had these mystics come back from Heaven to earth, when they felt it incumbent on them to teach mankind. They had to tell all men that the world perceived by the eyes of the body is doubtless real, but that there is something else, and that this something is no mere possibility or probability, like the conclusion of an argument, but the certainty of a thing experienced: here is one who has seen, who has touched, one who knows. And yet these were but the tentative beginnings of an apostolate. The enterprise was indeed discouraging: how could the conviction derived from an experience be handed down by speech? And, above all, how could the inexpressible be expressed? But these questions do not even present themselves to the great mystic. He has felt truth flowing into his soul from its fountainhead like an active force. He can no more help spreading it abroad than the sun can help diffusing its light. Only, it is not by mere words that he will spread it.

For the love which consumes him is no longer simply the love of man for God, it is the love of God for all men. Through God, in the strength of God, he loves all mankind with a divine love. This is not the fraternity enjoined on us by the philosophers in the name of reason, on the principle that all men share by birth in one rational essence: so noble an ideal cannot but command our respect; we may strive to the best of our ability to put it into practice, if it be not too irksome for the individual and the community; we shall never attach ourselves to it passionately. Or, if we do, it will be because we have breathed in some nook or corner of our civilization the intoxicating fragrance left there by mysticism. Would the philosophers themselves have laid down so confidently the principle, so little in keeping with everyday experience, of an equal participation of all men in a higher essence, if there had not been mystics to embrace all humanity in one simple indivisible love? This is not, then, that fraternity which started as an idea, whence an ideal has been erected. Neither is it the intensification of an innate sympathy of man for man. Indeed we may ask ourselves whether such an instinct ever existed elsewhere than in the imagination of philosophers, where it was devised for reasons of symmetry. With family, country, humanity appearing as wider and wider circles, they thought that man must naturally love humanity as he loves his country and his family, whereas in reality the family group and the social group are the only ones ordained by nature, the only ones corresponding to instincts, and the social instinct would be far more likely to prompt societies to struggle against one another than to unite to make up humanity. The utmost we can say is that family and social feeling may chance to overflow and to operate beyond its natural frontiers, with a kind of luxury value; it will never go very far. The mystic love of humanity is a very different thing. It is not the extension of an instinct, it does not originate in an idea. It is neither of the senses nor of the mind. It is of both, implicitly, and is effectively much more. For such a love lies at the very root of feeling and reason, as of all other things. Coinciding with God's love for His handiwork, a love which has been the source of everything, it would yield up, to anyone who knew how to question it, the secret of creation. It is still more metaphysical than moral in its essence. What it wants to do, with God's help, is to complete the creation of the human species and make of humanity what it would have straightaway become, had it been able to assume its final shape without the assistance of man himself. Or, to use words which mean, as we shall see, the same thing in different terms: its direction is exactly that of the vital impetus: it *is* this impetus itself, communicated in its entirety to exceptional men who in their turn would fain impart it to all humanity and by a living contradiction change into creative effort that created thing which is a species, and turn into movement what was, by definition, a stop. . . .